# BRAMAH'S
# QUEST

THE HEART of THIS JOURNEY · BEARS ALL PATTERNS ·

THOT J BAP

# BRAMAH'S QUEST

RENÉE SAROJINI SAKLIKAR

>>>>>>

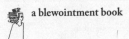

a blewointment book

NIGHTWOOD EDITIONS

2023

Nightwood Editions
P.O. Box 1779
Gibsons, BC VON 1V0
Canada
www.nightwoodeditions.com

COVER DESIGN: Topshelf Creative
COVER ART: Nadina Tandy
TYPOGRAPHY: Carleton Wilson

Nightwood Editions acknowledges the support of the Canada Council for the Arts, the
Government of Canada, and the Province of British Columbia through the BC Arts Council.

This book has been produced on 100% post-consumer recycled, ancient-forest-free paper,
processed chlorine-free and printed with vegetable-based dyes.

Printed and bound in Canada.

LIBRARY AND ARCHIVES CANADA CATALOGUING IN PUBLICATION

Title: Bramah's quest / Renée Sarojini Saklikar.
Names: Saklikar, Renée Sarojini, author.
Identifiers: Canadiana (print) 20220481849 | Canadiana (ebook) 20220481857 |
ISBN 9780889714304 (softcover) | ISBN 9780889714311 (EPUB)
Classification: LCC PS8637.A52 B75 2023 | DDC C811/.6—dc23

*Let all evil die and the good endure*

# CONTENTS

*Bramah Sojourns the Hidden Valley*

*The Young Raphael & His Story*

All Roads Lead to Paris: The Search for Bartholomew

PART TWO

*The Fall of Consortium in the Year 2105*

*Bartholomew & Raphael Join the Uprising*

*In Baghdad*

*Return to Paris, and Victory… Almost*

*The Short Rule of Bartholomew the Good*

*Civil War in the Wet*

The Restoration, 2108

Bramah at the Portal of the Lost Seasons

At the Gate of the Fisherman's Knot

♛

*Myth, story, legend, fact—*
*petals unfold together, apart.*
*Time's stem split, turned back,*
*the seasons, such riches, each twig and leaf,*
*threshold of discovery or precipice—*

# INTRODUCTION

*One afternoon, in an old house in an abandoned village on the outskirts of Perimeter, in the place they call Pacifica, Bramah and the Beggar Boy find fragments of an ancient text in an oak box.*

Thus began Book One of THOT J BAP and by the end, Bramah, a demigoddess trained as a locksmith, is forced to leave her adopted grandmother and the Beggar Boy they rescued, as well as the magic oak box they found, as she hurtles through a portal to the past on a mission to discover her own origins. In Book Two, *Bramah's Quest*, her mission continues: she searches not only for her story, but also for her people—helping Seed Savers and resisters battle against the evil Consortium in a world ever more devastated by climate change and global inequality.

If the beating heart of Book One was the parchment-scroll story of the ill-fated Dr. A.E. Anderson and her adopted daughter Abigail, at the centre of Book Two is the love affair between Abigail's son Raphael and the Warrior General Sherronda who helps wrest victory away from Consortium, at least for a brief while.

THOT J BAP is:

**Epic** in that it is long: each book is a poem and there are several books that comprise the series. And epic in that the themes are broad and deep, and include the battle between good and evil, and the choices humans must make between desire and necessity.

**Fantasy** in that there is time travel, shape-shifting, magic realism. Many things happen, some good, mostly bad, including five eco-catastrophes and yes, a bio-contagion (pandemic).

**Verse** in that the story is told through poetic forms often used in the epic: blank verse, cantos, sonnets, madrigals, chants, ballads, spells and codes, as well as the merging of these traditional forms with my signature docu-poetics where the language of reportage and historical texts is mimicked and repurposed for the long poem.

Most of all, this book contains the lives lived by characters caught up in cataclysmic events, where individual heartache, love and loss take place on a ravaged earth. There's even a little hope—in the kindness of the locksmith Bramah as she tries to save humankind from itself, and in the actions of the craftspeople making things to help humans survive.

*Bramah's Quest*—shall we begin?

## CHARACTERS

**Bramah**: an English/Indian (South Asian) locksmith, demigoddess and hero of the saga. Her motto is *Let All Evil Die and the Good Endure.* She is on a quest to find her people and her origins.

**Bartholomew**: a scholar radicalized by the Resistance. Reluctant leader. Lover of the late Abigail who perished in Book One.

**Raphael**: the son of Bartholomew and Abigail.

**Sherronda**: Warrior General and skilled commander of the Resistance. (Her real name is *Shanti-Ben*, given to her by the Aunties who found her on a barren heath between the Wet and the Dry. Shanti-Ben means Sister of Peace). She wields the Sword of Kali and all who feel that blade die.

**Bramah's Grandmother**: a storyteller and mendicant. She is a matriarch of the Resistance and adopts orphans.

**The Beggar Boy**: Bramah's apprentice. Both he and Grandmother were separated from Bramah in Book One.

**Consortium**: a global industrial, economic, agricultural and communications mega-corporation on the verge of collapse due to the effects of accelerated climate change. It still controls access to the electrical grid known as the Big E.

**Guards of the Fifth Gate**: specialists in Surveillance. Foot soldiers and mercenaries, they hire on with Bartholomew due to hunger and lack of wages.

**Rajancrantz & Gabbarbhai**: two Gujarati assassins loyal to Sherronda. She secretly hires them as a wartime film crew.

**Women of the Wishing Well**: mendicant midwives who live over a hundred years, these aunties are matriarchs of a network of survivors and resisters. In this book we hear of Aunty Magda and Aunty Tabitha.

**Beggars**: displaced orphans, often indentured as labourers. Their rhymes and chants, songs and slogans, often act as an underground communications system to which Bramah always pays attention.

**Swords**: well-bred, rebellious fighters banished by Consortium for misdemeanours then recruited by Bramah. Famous for their smarts and weapon skills, they are at odds with the Warrior General Sherronda.

**The Magnolia Brigade**: textile workers, both skilled and unskilled, liberated by Sherronda from the free trade zones of Consortium. They are fierce fighters totally loyal to Sherronda.

**T-LOHK**: an itinerant scribe. She appears/disappears, sojourning with Seed Savers and resisters.

**Ciswen, Blacksmith of the Winter Portal**: she makes Bramah's locksmith tools.

All characters are uninvited settlers on the unceded territories, the world over, of First Peoples.

## LOCATIONS

**Consortium**: an integrated global economic and administrative empire, covering most of the known world and controlling all aspects of industry, agriculture and food production. In this book, accelerated climate change disrupts the supply lines crucial to Consortium's hold on the world and its power weakens.

**Cities**: these include the Great Cities of Transaction: Paris, Baghdad and Ahmedabad.

**Perimeter**: cities and settlements fortified and controlled by Consortium. Rentalsman is an agency of Perimeter.

**Towers and Gates**: this is where the guards and agents of Consortium control who can enter and exit Perimeter.

**Portal Gates to the Four Seasons**: these are found in different locations outside Perimeter. Although the portals are controlled by Consortium, if you happen to know the right spells, as Bramah does, the portals can act as departure points for time travel. In this book, the Four Seasons are ravaged by accelerated climate change, decaying into brutal cold dry, hot dry and the Wet.

**Pacifica**: a region extending from the western, ocean side, of a continent once known as America.

# PART ONE

*Broken on Its Hinge, the Winter Portal, 2087*

## ORACLE, UNHEEDED

Didn't I tell you? Didn't I?
Faster and faster, birds and seeds.
No ship will save you,
no end to your misdeeds.

No parchment in hand to bolster belief.
No explanation to satisfy grief.
Only an old oak box, found and then lost.

Didn't I shelter him, that Beggar Boy?
No journey too cold, no warning too bright.
Only an old woman, brown skin unlined.
Only our Bramah, to search and then find.

Didn't I tell you, didn't I?
Ah yes, you rose up, your seeds and your glass.
Didn't I warn you though?
Faster and faster, oceans to ice age,
oxygen depleted, nowhere to breathe.

Throw nine shells down, find any runes left.
Snow covered, four sepals, one pistil, saved.
*Un coup de dés, jamais, jamais*
Didn't I tell you, after each story lost
there's another to be found only if
*Un coup de dés*——

## ABANDONED AT THE WISHING WELL

Aunties of the Four
*Winter, Spring and Fall*
in the Dry, cracked soil
*Summer all enraged—*

Winter, Spring and Fall
*in the Wet, drowning*
Aunties of the Four
*Summer but a dream*

*Stir and Blend,* they cried
warmer rising tall
Winter, Spring and Fall
*never in the end*

Aunties of the Four
*cracked soil, drowning wet*
faster and faster
*the End of the Four.*


>>>>>>
♕ ♕ ♕
>>>>>>


And we, ghost survivors from the Before
        martyred Seed Savers, migrants
            guild workers, banned.
*Un coup de dés, jamais, jamais.*

*Drought, drought so scorching*
*we longed for deluge*
*thick, torrential, heavy and wet.*
*When the Wet came, deluge driven,*
*we longed for sun, not scorching*
*benign warm fingers to grow and heal.*
*The Wet and the Dry didn't listen.*

From far and away
      heard distant and echoing
warriors who coughed as they kicked the dust
      singing, they marched eastward.
*Spruce, chestnut, two cherry trees and six oaks*
*a plane tree and a beech—once was a house.*
One soldier stopped and rubbed the well's stone rim,
      slate tiles inlaid into granite, chiselled,
*Et in Arcadia ego.*
Not everyone laughed.


>>>>>>
♕ ♕ ♕
>>>>>>

## ACCELERATED AND DECAYED

*More viruses jumping between species.*
We whispered warnings, no one left to heed.
Molten underneath, ocean floor slip-strike.
A thousand kilometres north to north,
tectonic moving toward, shoved under

locked, stored up in rock awaiting the Great Day,
our feet no farther than lava, flumes flowed.
*Behind us the wall,* captured children scrawled,
*to buckle and then to let go.*
Every single year, hotter and hotter,
secret schools to repair and to grow, plants
scarce, food shortages worse, prices up, up:
*Currency notes, gold, obsolete?* we asked.
*No,* gold stayed hoarded, armed guards, locked-away vaults.
Graffiti from paint-squeezed red madder plants:
locked, we move toward, hundreds of years, pull!
Quick, low tide to high tide in minutes.
Decades after, ferocious winds, ozone
gaps in the sky, warnings, drought to famine
　　　　famine to war, this is how it was then.

And Bramah entered——
oak box multiples, revealing the past.
Consortium contracts, filched first to last,
profits declining with each winter's end.
If nuclear, then "only limited,"
or so said Consortium managers.
Time's memory, a wicker basket, pulled, frayed:
*Nasty, brutish, short,* cried Beggars to Swords.
Bramah stopped to listen, always searching
that gap-toothed grin, or a broken shoelace——

Peering close, she'd wonder, are you the one?
Children shook their heads, *No*, then ran away.

*No one could have foreseen*, we said, walking
away from our old lives, sad and resigned.
*Would the Before-Time come back?* we asked her.
Answering with her feet, Bramah urged us
ever forward.

## BRAMAH'S ARRIVAL

Our mouths opened without sound
      we jumped back
to see her tumble in
      black braids, head frosted
Pippin file flung to the ice-crusted ground.

We ran to her, Winter's Portal closing
our breath hung in the air and then——

She could elide time, head bent to her task
fingers on the knob of a lock; click, turn.
One day under the watch of the Fifth Gate
Guards called in to supervise all of us,
her chanted words barely heard under breath
images rose, our minds flooded with green,
emerald fields, clear lakes, crystal streams, fresh runs
we swallowed longing, tilted back our heads
temperate forests, the likes we'd never seen.

Called into Rentalsman she told us true
code to key, then turn your water Geiger
set the counter to zero, mind you save
as much as you can, peak flow times
daily to once weekly, bucket to tap
five stamps to one card, keep track of the dates
forget how you used to live, learn new ways
thimble to cup, lash to tongue, mark your days.

In the street that time forgot, three black cats
Bramah walked—sure-footed hero, her satchel swinging
a crowd of urchins, not yet grown to mob,
      trailing behind her, studying her moves.

Every time her fingers touched inscription
engraved edges, rough curves to her thumb's edge
origin and incident, loose binding
shaken by the centrefold, Bramah jumped
fences, gates, seasons, stars, laughter and tears.

♛

She was heard to say these words while working:

*Elusive story, my past pulled skin first*
*Kingsway, once a place all my little finds*
*traffic jammed at Aberdeen and Wessex.*
*We'd laugh, settler names, embroidered falseness*
*our school uniforms, donated by the state.*

Understand, this were the dead of winter
still she warned of the Dry to come, harsh times,
dense fabric of outer world edges, pulled.
*Fix the roof while the sun is shining*
Bramah's words remembered with rueful smiles.
Wet to Dry, the cycle of the Seasons
not much we could count on, except the wars.
Sharp pokes from the Fear God, empty cupboards.
We recounted hidden packets of saved seeds.
We learned to scavenge, mended broken things.
Joy came with repair. Although forbidden.
Consortium dictated our methods' heresy.
Hidden Valley Guilds, light portals away.
Some of us believed in history, some prayed.
None yet willing to accept times as these.

The thing about Bramah, she gave us hope:
she taught us trees, branch and bark, our meeting
secured by cedar or spruce, beech or oak
imported for years or native species.
She taught us messages, relayed from their roots,
thin stripes of grey in the heart of red stone.
*Settlers, all of us,* she'd warn, *earn our keep.*
Not wanted here, yet here we found ourselves.
Old Autumn Portal seldom used,
windows shuttered, doors locked, streets deserted
except Tower Juniper balconies—
concrete eroded, dark water stains, mould...
She jumped up to the second floor, pushed
open Rentalsman, vagabond children:

*Jumped the Fence, did you?*
*We did, too.*

Pinched faces, staring eyes, still they stood proud.
*I am here,* Bramah said. *All will be well.*
We held our heads low; we didn't dare tell.

## BRAMAH SEARCHES FOR CISWEN, BLACKSMITH OF THE WINTER PORTAL

First, a long chain of migrants;
     after the Battle of Kingsway
after earthquakes, fires, hurricanes blown
     earth ripped, scorched, city towers collapsed, cables
exposed: the Big E setbacks abolished
     homes flooded, rebuilt by Consortium
and the asking price, only to obey.
     Unshed tears lined their bellies, their throats tight
sadness a substance, coating their tongues white.

Second, I sojourned, helping out when I could
     and then the river was taken away and that night
I kneeled, cold damp seeping into my bones
*How might I find Ciswen, the blacksmith?* I asked the Moon.

And the Moon told me instead
     this story:

     Eve of Eves, when beasts would speak, they'd kneel
     river mornings, mist lifting, trace memories;
     iron worker, she searched for base metals.
     *Everyone can use a tool.* She smiled sweet.
     Good with fire, for years she shunned beauty,
     unaware of her own, choosing to weld
     desert visions a thousand miles away.
     Red earth, red stone, she learned, made her own tongs
     out of granite, mica flecks, wide hips formed,
     her copper chain necklace, thin links adorned
     by map and by clock, the sweat of her brow,
     mosaic, a thousand droplets, distilled.

Each a mirror, revealed to her, a forge,
river's edge, high meadow, four-cornered road.

I knew then to stay on the path.

♛

# BRAMAH FINDS CISWEN AND HEARS PROPHECY

Knives, swords, silver daggers, hammer, anvil:
Ciswen crafted metals, worked wooden handles
rock, bone, flint to copper, iron and steel,
herself the worker, or scavenged premade
flat bars smuggled; Consortium guards bribed.
Power hammers, electric grinders, too.
Beggars and Swords stole for her, abandoned coal.
Tongs and bellows to stoke her fire, anvil
cast, her control of the grain, steel prowess.
To heat the blade, then to quench it in oil.
Strong state, polished with emery, fingers
bled to sharpen, her ancient whetstone.
She made her own hammer and anvil, tongs
two pairs sized thin to thick, upright iron vise,
famed for Damascus blades, November's curse.
Seasons from the Before-Time marked the dark.
Ciswen taught me not just craft but spell, too.
When a southeast wind blew *Pacifica*
Ciswen taught me, right as rain, good as new.
Blonde braids flying, she'd cry, *Bramah, head north.*
Find the true place, hunker down there, wait days
learn patience, that's the secret to the blade——

*A forge to shape our past,* I learned to say.
Months later when Consortium fell, I marched.
Beggars and Swords at my side, Ciswen disappeared.
For now, though, we knew nothing of such things.
Threshold survivors, heading on our quest.

*Bramah,* said Ciswen, *you'll have to be tested.
Every hero ever was. You'll have to travel, portals
to place and back again, Spain to India, Rome to Khyber*

*Pacifica roamer, transport plane dodger, overland and then*
*to Baghdad, courtyard inside the Green Zone*
*Ahmedabad, those factory floors swept clean.*
*Bramah,* said Ciswen, *I'll make you the finest tools.*
*Pippin file and plier, pick, key and lock.*
*I'll beat silver and lead, I'll smelt iron and forge steel.*
*But you'll need visions, too, to find the right spells.*
And then did Ciswen make these things? She did.
And my quest for Raphael continued.

♛

## THE WET AND THE DRY

Wind voices howled in jest, we coughed, crouched low
  *Goodbye temperate*
  *Hello extreme, rise!*

Still for many a day, into months, years,
roaming brigands, refugees, Seed Savers
sang to both seasons, hoping to placate
worse things from happening:

*Come in from the Wet, let go your regret,*
sodden voices echoed, mud-splattered rags
tied up to their knees, Beggars and Swords sighed,
brooms traded for shovels, sandbag fillers,
Guards of the Fifth, long-deserted convoys,
no longer anyone to point a gun.
Yet still they dug trenches, water released.
*Layer us,* each boy called. *We'll swim for you.*
Stranded dockside, a thousand containers
broken and mildewed, we squatted inside.
*Now, Bartholomew,* we murmured, *find us.*
*Here, Bramah, work your magic, bring us the sun.*
*Dry rays to lift skies, ultraviolet:*
*recede these waters, bring us the Dry.*

Decaying, those schoolroom walls fell inward.
Each day a year long, rain dropped unceasing.
Where once four, now only two arriving:
shape-shifters, limbs bendy, capable of—
Crossing that river, they gazed far below
epoch workers, those steel structures, strong bridge
between sectors, sentries, automatic
rifles slung sideways; uniforms bartered—

Inside that one schoolroom, teachers sang, *Let's*
*just see what tomorrow brings.* Rain falling,
sun pulses behind grey skies, days counted,
seated centre-left, cross-legged, Bramah said,
*Take your time with things, study how they work.*
Round key notched, surface metal slides, opening——

# THE SIFTING SISTERS AT THE OLD WELL

They believed in handwritten fragments:
papers or art, the made thing, hand to touch
cotton, linen, vellum, foolscap, cheap notebooks
scribbled grocery store lists, old pamphlets
sticky notes, index cards, once a lifetime
over and through those hard years descending.
Aura and emanations, words to stroke
fingertips brushing stained raglan, cardboard
circling, rubbing, eyes closed, hands to touch words—

All things must fade, pass away and return
          green shoots, old wood, acacia, laurel
winter flowering jasmine, glossy leaves
          luck-bearer if we but pay attention
how to recede from the centre with grace
          who will be left to listen to earth-words
sent in every windstorm, quake, fire, flood
          all things must fade then pass away, return
bring sweet flowering jasmine for good luck
          chance and fate will meet us at this last gate.
Then these two wizened Aunties each proclaimed:

> *Hurry your search Bramah, green and golden,*
>           *Abigail's boy has forgotten his father.*
> *Find the Valley, you'll find them both*
>           *find the Seasons, you'll love them most.*
> *Green and golden, Bramah, seed and settler*
>           *your quest will be longer, your deeds far known.*
>           *acorn to fence, chalice to chess, fare forward!*

Bramah shrugged off the words of these sisters.
Head down, unsmiling, she trekked eastward.

>>>>>>

# Bramah on the Trail of Raphael

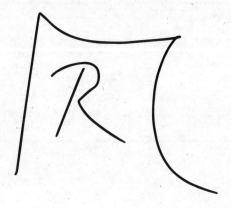

# GHOST SETTLERS AT THE GATE

Icy air, heavy fog, she shrugged off cold:
sleeveless tunic, her shoulders rosy-gold.
Thrown into the Winter Portal headfirst,
she brought with her orphans crying their thirst.

Unbinder of knots, crooked things made straight
broken locks repaired, cast-off finds salvaged
objects held, turned for their use potential;
cracks sealed, duct tape saved, Before-Time gears greased.
Wrench to plier, turntable to CD,
canny to barter for Big E rations.
Click, jiggle, rasp and saw, she made things work—
codes recited at the drop of a hat.
*Smooth fixer*, we said, no doubt about that.

Elliptical, always spinning forward,
parchment-scroll fragments, dust-covered oak box
Bramah's arrival, Ciswen at the helm
locksmith and blacksmith on the hunt for us.
At the Gate of Ice and Doom, Ciswen left
called by the All Mother elsewhere, forge ready——
We would lead her to the boy Raphael.

Each word when spoken leapt from mouth to soil
curlicues and upward strokes, root and flower.
Month's end a precipice, portal gaping——
*Bramah*, we urged, *unlock each Season's Gate.*
    *Find the boy and the father, don't be late.*

## FIRST, THE GREAT VAULT

Everything locked away, codes, passwords, charms:
digital, titanium, gold or steel.
Bramah's fingers nimble, turn, file, click, guess.
Consortium hired her till month's end,
each year's contract fulfilled. Her face quite blank;
when questioned about resisters, she'd smile.
Spies, drones to monitor her every move.
Uncanny, how often her guess proved right,
all those guns no use, try as soldiers might
to outmanoeuvre her deft strategies—
to hide always, smooth-faced and in plain sight.
Time and again we saw her give them the slip,
we heard her voice before we saw her steps.
Sure-footed, snow waist-high, or fording streams.

*Sakura*, Bramah would say, then, *dogwood.*
*Jump the Fence, roll the dice, find the oak trees—*
Long after she'd left for another job
we, hidden, unseen by drones or by men
inscribed, engraved, etched, carved, traced all her words:
Hidden Valley shimmering between worlds,
banyan to maple, cotton to silk, luck!

## Bramah's Questing Song as She Worked on Hire for Consortium

Sakura, dogwood, magnolia too
Peony to roses, faraway spring
Once lush, green, elderberry by solstice
Blossom to cup, bud to petal falling
Order and sequence, aligned, once we were—
*Un coup de dés, jamais, jamais*

♛ ♛ ♛


Golden key in Bramah's hands unlocking
*tales within tales, chalice,* the old well sighed.
How the bees hummed with Bramah's fingers, quick,
turning to click, then run, to find again—

## THEN, OVERHEARD IN A BODEGÓNE

Over her left shoulder, bright crescent moon
she was to meet Memory and Desire.

Rubbed, held, discarded—
lamp lit, door open
two bodies glistening, oiled rhythm in-out:

upstairs in that old tavern, wild men bought—
*'Cause you know I've been spying on your life.*

She laughed low, those two unsmoked cigarettes
tucked upright, front shirt pocket, green army-

issued, stolen, worn for two centuries.
April Portal, open: all she needed—

to be at the gates at noon or midnight.
*'Cause I want to, and feel that I must*

*dispel bad dreams, Voyager!* Forward ever faring—
*No sign yet of the boy, Raphael,* we said.

## THROUGH THE TIMEKEEPER'S HALL

Clocks of every kind imaginable shelved.
Calendars, ripped pages, piles stacked.
Sundials under skylights, shafted circles.
Archival drawers, soft cambric cloth pinned.
Artifacts of the Seasons as once were:
green acorns turned to golden brown, waxed leaves.
Sakura blossoms transparent with dust.
Ice blocks, sawdust strewn, miraculously
still frozen—small pools of meltwater under her hands—
Separate chambers for the storage of seeds.
Row upon row of mason jars, labelled.
Beans, tomatoes, apples, squash, corn and wheat.
Not a spot of mould, no rot, all clean, neat.
Herbs in packets, tree roots preserved in boxes.
Fragments of books since the Gutenberg press.
Tin boxes, compass sets from the Before.
Hoards of dictionaries, obsolete now.
One Apple IIe computer, unplugged.
Six pedestals, home to huge parchment scrolls.
Handwritten and illuminated hours:
the names of every species lost; tear-stained.

# SIDETRACKED BY CONSORTIUM

That day Consortium containers lost,
error code messages accumulating.
Supply chain delays, device part mislaid.
Every lockbox she touched, the key broke first.
Jammed, metal files rasped, dull and useless. Still,
she worked Pippin and tweezers, picking——
Reset codes by guessing sequences, click,
turn, and turn again, drops of sweat fell slick.
Still she crouched, eye lifting, preset timers
click, blink, drip, still her brown fingers steady.
When all else failed, she knew a set of spells:
*Numbers and signs,* she'd whisper, *now unwind.*
Delays and shortages, mishaps and spades—
bad cards, she turned luck, all her contracts made.

And quick, just in the nick of time, she'd flee,
she'd figure things out, she'd map her path
sure-footed and alert, she'd spy her chance
no matter which portal gate. She'd look once,
eyes intaking, the lay of the land known—
*Trust the rise of hills, the slant of footpaths*
*count escalators and memorize halls—*
no place foreign to her steady brown gaze.
*Un coup de dés,* Bramah sang as she ran.
In this way she earned her keep, kept searching.

# RENDEZVOUS WITH THE SCRIBE T-LOHK

In a tavern frequented by resisters and Seed Savers—
*Every uprising needs a meeting place,*
this they all said and laughed—Consortium
drones darting, satellites jammed and roaming.
Snug room and a lineup, papers in hand.
They waited to get their stories inscribed.
Flickering light of three beeswax candles,
dip, write, blow, blot, she rarely raised her head.
Those closer peered down, India ink script
rich, measured, dense, exact, then broken:
either a quill split or her pen ran out—
Parchment scraps, scraped vellum reused; receipts—
Slippery scrolls, ripped edges, pencil and pen.
FRAGILE HANDLE WITH CARE labels and paste;
tape rolls at the half, foolscap by the pound,
rare paper worth its weight in gold, so scarce.
Hoarded, stolen, bartered, kept for decades.
Pencil ends, quill bits, micro-lead spokes stacked.
Vials of plastic from the Before-Time, cleared space.

T-LOHK, Itinerant Scribe, seated and writing
words for hire, Seed Savers paid in kind.
Survivor letters posted, Cy-Board #6.
Bramah smiled and kept her distance, watching:
T-LOHK's ink pen, remediated quill
flowing across a page, words-a-sighting.
*Last Time I Ever Saw Your Face,* she wrote,
woman at the edge, Lost Seasons Portal:

sodden grey skies, a slice of lemon light
far-edged, Perimeter documented
margins, a small script, inked handwriting, clear.
*Once and Used to Be*, title for her song.


>>>>>>

# BRAMAH READS T-LOHK'S INSCRIPTIONS

At first light, T-LOHK set out, no goodbyes.
She left a set of parchments for Bramah.


### i. *Tale of the Girl from the Magnolia Brigade*

I remember the sound of his voice, deep
rough, ragged, he asked me to write
into his black book, cream pages, smooth leather
bound and unlined, soft to the touch.
I wrote my name with his pen, our fingers——
Not a sign nor a word from him since then,
once Guard of the Fifth Gate, stone-cold blue eyes.
Once were the October Portal where we first met
opening to chance, *Un coup de dés*—
Wind swept city, rain without burning, leaves
imprinting their light-shaped weight on cement.


### ii. *Tale of the Un/Named Farm Labourer, Consortium Hire*

We heard two explosions down by the dock.
Albion Ferry refugees come up,
them living under the bridge, their children.
They left two boys with me, Ahmad and Jake.
I brought them up as brothers as we saved seeds.
*Allium sativum, Solanum* too.
Guards pounding on our door—and me, ironing
washing clothes for Perimeter mansions.
That day, we fled out the back door yelling
*Ma, don't try and save me!* and Ahmad struck
iron to the face of one of the Guards.
We made camp the night after, river's edge
joined the long lines searching for food, shelter—

### iii. Tale of the Iron Mistress, Magnolia Brigade

After they raped our sisters, we rose up
armed with cast-off guns and swords, we butchered.
Hacked off heads and legs, blood spattered aprons
cleaning ourselves with river sand, we washed.
We scavenged Perimeter families,
them with their evo cars and their imports,
online ordering, fine linens, the best.
One-thousand-thread-count sheets, we stole, laundered—
many uses for cotton and rayon.
Patch 'n Mend, hiss of steam, of press and sew.
Before-Time ration cards bartered for wood.
We found cast iron, stoves and kettles whistling,
sparks from the heat loved by all who gathered.
Them tools! To fit a woman's hand, demanding
plenty of muscle to lift, scrub washboards
warm metal on white flannel, wet to dry
our hair, steam frizzed, our cheeks flushed
we sang of rain, unburning, after months,
dry soil dampened after drought; fingers singed.

### iv. Tale of the Un/Known Woman Soldier

All her battles fought yet unacknowledged.
Cast out from Perimeter, scorned looks thrown,
she entrusted me with these Moon-Side songs:

> Of many losses, your colloidal face
> scars turned to night-river reflections, fierce
> polluted waters, effluent, old mills
> speaking in an undertow dialect.
> Of many losses, your sly grinning face

shredding clouds, rushing against that other
face that is no face, far future, oak box
blackened with trouble, ground into granite
empty and full, filled with discarded dreams.
My heart, no cedar-lined hope chest, chambers
empty and full, fragrance, lost seasons call
words into signs, six-sided, pushing waves
time's current forward, back, of many lost.
Yellow-grey river eye, your baleful stare.
Your laughing waters, your scorn drifts down here.

## *v. T-LOHK's Own Tale of the Beggars*

Waiting for Bramah they recited songs
welcoming themselves into hostile space,
*Brandywine Ferry, Buckleberry bridge.*
How they laughed, voices hoarse to sing these words,
lost. October Portal, the rains poured down.
Consortium unable to control.
Approved builders, extravagant displays
*Showtime!* cried the boys; I slipped away.
Sub-corporation directors, seated
select families invited, three tiers;
access to London, Paris, Tokyo
sedate and restrained in their luxury.
Electric cars, no plastic bags, eco-
correct. Outside, under the bridge we stood
                          —shivering.
Grandma taught us how to keep going.
*Hostile faces, unreceptive spaces,*
she'd laugh and say, *Learn to welcome yourself.*

## vi. Tale of the Sword Turned Seed Saver

As a child I was obsessed with safety, security and secrets.
And magic, and walking to the river where I'd run
skipping stones, leaping over tires at night set to fire—
then to the culvert, it were after the Battle of Kingsway.
Safe house what some called Manse, large yellow brick-
walled garden, hidden door, honey locust trees brushing.
There to find tacked to the Seed Savers' hut,
a Shiva calendar: turned the pages
counted sixty-four, each page a move, checked
against replications, old books on chess,
each square contained a warning about change,
the kind we found ourselves in, drought and floods.
Ground ozone, knight takes bishop, save the queen.
East Antarctic Ice Sheet, protected pass.
Climate change, checkmate. Prophecy or Fate.
Each page, an image: chalice or oak box.
Words touched my fingertips and whispered songs
barely audible, something about a beggar boy
thrown into a rogue portal, transponder
emanating vibrations, Great Year calling:
*Un coup de dés, Vega to Draco, jump!*

♛

Bramah, who could read upside down quite well,
leapt up and placed her hand on T-LOHK's arm
quill pen down with a splash of ink and then——

Bramah dropped to her knee and traced these words,
fingertip to carved letters, they faded:

*B is for Bramah, foot first at the Gate.*
*B is for Beauty, always your true Fate.*

34

## BRAMAH AND THE OAK BOX

If oak, then from which forest, acorns split.
The cap oval, teardrop-shape saved.
Tiny protrusion, small circle indents.
Tam o' Shanter lid, stick handle, chevrons
over-layered skin, nut hard rolling bounce.

If a box, then whose hands to carve to join,
not one nail, each side fit, groove to the end.
If magic, then wood to metal and back,
bronze, copper, iron, to gold, to oak.

If touched by evil hands, then nothing seen
save to lure, by deceit or design, false
fortunes, stray paths, grandiose schemes gone wrong.
If touched by Bramah, then small things, deep roots,
dried marigold heads, sweet pungent and rubbed.

*Quercus*, Bramah laughed, addressing the box,
*I've finally found you again! Speak now,*
*tell me where I might find and what to bring.*
*Catkin to cupule, my origins tell.*

When Bramah placed her hands again inside
her fingers brushed only the smooth wood planks.
Instead of prophecy, at first silence,
hands on the hinged lid, her ear to the side:

*Water and shade, whispered Beggars and Swords,*
*conscripted to dig dry soil, smoke-filled winds.*
*Raphael is hidden, that boy you seek, gone.*

## BRAMAH AT THE BEACH HEAD WITH HER KEEPSAKE

Worn almost to invisible, her key
gold filigree, mere thing, yet bonded strong.
She could make it unlock a thousand doors.
Gates on their hinges, copper-iron swing,
back and forth, to let in the Wet and the Dry——

No human to convey, only lost sounds.
Name after name rose up from the ocean,
seaweed strands wound around extinct species.
Bramah fell to her knees on the hard sand,
not the animals themselves but their names
codified classification in script
dripping wet Latin genus to family
infinite list, rising from placid waves.
Tears caught in Bramah's lashes; acorns palmed.
Kelp gatherers pointed, high crumbling cliffs
seagulls, raucous, reeled against torn grey skies.
A giant fern, sans serif, towering,
*Carnian and pluvial,* each stroke sighed.
Bramah shook her head, brown eyes widening.

Behind her, the parched continent burning
dried grass, dead trees, diesel-soaked air, dead bees.

At the place of the chasm, an Ancient:
*Never forget,* they whispered with blue-parched lips,
*the fiery sadness that is desire.*

And Bramah said, *Old Crone, I'll run from your bony hands.*
Before she could escape, that dry voice croaked,
*When we were all together, hot and dry,*
*no flowers, grasses or birds, not even us!*

By now Bramah pounded away on the hard sands.
*Pangaea,* cried the old crone, *remember!*
Mid-stride, Bramah stopped, then ran back panting.
    *Old One. You forgot to tell me*
      *about the boy.*
Coughing and laughing, the Ancient took hours—
    a long tale about quests and searching hearts.

# BRAMAH LEARNS OF RAPHAEL & THE HIDDEN VALLEY

Tossing and turning on cold, hard ground,
ancient dreamscapes, kaleidoscopic rolls
unfurling, they whispered, *Pay attention!*

> the year 1784—carved arm—
> her left muscle raised,
> each child around her

> stunted, Vitamin D deficient,
> they'd learned to adapt,
> kept hidden from those guards—

They unspooled memory, tales, story-travels,
portal-hopping, her chants and spells, intact.
Ancient voices, they plied Bramah's mind:
ghost presences of the Four Seasons left,
faint tracks of what once was winter, spring, fall—
        summer everywhere, one long drought.
Ghost voices leading Bramah to Makers,
deep inside the Hidden Valley, unseen—

*The Tale of the Lost Makers*

In this way, Bramah journeyed to hear us:
Perimeter spy, Consortium contract worker.
Bramah met us at the House of the Glass Makers.
She made us sit and wait before leaving.
She told us of the good doctor, now dead.
She recited passages of time travel,
there and back, to find a chalice:
this is what they called *microscopes*—
the name forbidden. So many things were.

We agreed to show her our secret map.
We told her to leave at the break of dawn:
*Follow the morning star ever eastward*
*Hidden Valley of the Shimmering Oaks:*
how we smiled sharing these words and memories.
Warmed breath trapped by our masks, we pointed true:
>*When you find the Makers' Circle,*
>*you'll find him too.*
>*Raphael the lost boy, hidden in oak*
>>*shimmering leaves—*
At night in her dreams, close enough to touch
golden acorn, throat's hollow, luck-bearer
bead given to her by Grandmother when—
Transmission interrupted by the wind
roaring across abandoned encampments.
Bramah left us at first light, walking fast.
Mind's eye remembering strong hands to braid
without a pull or a tug, smooth and oiled,
three thick black plaits, one golden acorn clasp.

♛

Hidden Valley trail, months later
found by Guards deserting Consortium.
>Parchment scraps, lines written
>>it was said, by T-LOHK, the Itinerant Scribe,
>>attributed to Bramah:

>*This burden, frailty, I carry lonely*
>*past the North Star, through the Lost Seasons Gate.*
>*Black ribbons and green cypress, bowls of salt,*
>*words to win us a thousand years, I'm told—*
>*How can I explain the messages sent?*
>*Light falling slant across my cheek and hair;*

*inked fingers, translating from the Before,*
*cedar grove or dusty culvert, streetside*
*kneeling on green, my head bowed to receive.*

>>>>>>

# Bramah Sojourns the Hidden Valley

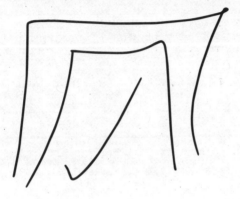

# BRAMAH AT THE SHIMMERING OAKS

She looked down at the map we'd drawn and smiled.
Fingers traced each twist and turn of the road;
mere path, once straight as a city street
running northeast, bounded by two highways.
Messages at first faint, tapped Autumn's Gate
since crumbling of Consortium locked:
Bramah's keys burnished to work with her spells
to get from the Dry to the Wet, urgent.
She knew the ship we came in on, waited
only the span of a year's worth of days,
one huge chestnut, three oaks, stunted plane trees,
old Consortium calendars and clocks
still used after a fashion. Month's end meeting,
many wouldn't notice our group,
not invisible, exactly: unseen.
Potters, woodcarvers, painters, glass-blowers,
tinsmiths, weavers, dyers, basket makers.
Our wares stored under blankets and rugs.
Grandmother knew us and told us to send
embedded messages to Raphael,
indentured to Consortium Concrete.
      We made things:
goblets, key boxes, glazed plates, Mason jars.
Cooking pots, tapestries, baskets and bread.
Our delight to figure out transmission:
         warnings and messages.
A twist of dough, pastry-letters, baked, glazed.
Stitched names hidden under cotton's rough fold.
Acid to etch, ash lye to wash, copper—
Look to the bottom! We'd laugh, ovens, hot.
Alive by the touch of hands who made
wheel to loom, honeycomb to lathe, forged, carved,

carded, pulled, stretched, tilled, planted, dried, saved.
*If by oil on canvas, if by mud thrown!*
Bramah smiled at these words and asked us straight,
*Now, have any of you seen my grandmother?*
We shook our heads side to side and told her
what she already knew. She said, *Tell me again.*
*Let me hear once more the story of our people.*

# GRANDMOTHER'S ORIGIN STORY

We called her Myriam from Jitali
*Gujarati-bolo?* she'd ask us slantwise,
Masala Queen who read from her *kitab*.
She'd laugh in the face of *Where you from?* blues.
She brought no dowry, but red earth saved.
Glass jars stacked in a jewelled cart pulled slow.
Four water buffalo, butter churned fresh.
Renowned beauty, deft with needle and thread.
Three Oxford firsts, expert with a rifle.
*Munay Bo Majah Ché.* She laughed, cursing
guards with guns and Consortium orders.
Parlay adapter, she negotiated
safe relocation of her buffalo:
riches aplenty for First World transfers.
Years spent working kiosks, Yonge Street at Bloor.
*Oceanside vacation,* Myriam sang.
Black hair streaked grey, brown legs running fast, free.

No one dared call her Grandmother at all.
PhD sharpshooter, heeding the call:
a thousand cross-continental journeys.
Friday prayer rituals. After, brewed chai.
Cherrywood tabla, magical lyrics.
In this way she stayed forever lithe, young.
Savings used to buy a settler's homestead.
Investments in a restaurant she named
Dogma Is a Mule. She raised a fortune,
funded scholarships for young poet girls'
recitations at midnight, fierce stories.
*Be your own mythmaker,* Myriam sang.
We'd last heard from her just before the Shift:
seasons destroyed into the Dry, the Wet.

Caravanserai traders said she lived
past the Valley of the Shimmering Oaks.
Outside Perimeter, still resisting——
Solstice to solstice, Grandmother appeared:
*Makers! Stay close to the fire, the rose.*
Grandmother's magic, to hide in plain view.
To find the boy for he held the chalice
piece from the Before-Time, saved, tucked away.
From the wheel and the forge, a set of tools
buried at the base of the old oak tree:
Pippin file, screwdriver, plier and pick.
*We keep them for my granddaughter,* she said.
Potters, woodcutters, code breakers, migrants,
arrivals to the circle, she taught us:

> *gold, silver, iron, bronze*
> > *steel and titanium*
> *rosemary and devil's wort*
> > *bind and bane*
> *let all evil die and the good endure.*


Refugees flooded in,
Grandmother brought them to Ciswen at the Forge.

Ragtag remnant cult, their hymns scant and rare.
*Like the stars in the morning,* they sang. Sweet
verses where once-mighty stone cathedrals stood.
God of Dominion, who sacrificed Earth.
The All Mother took pity on their plight.
She found them heartsore in the Hidden Valley—
Bread makers, their ovens marked with a cross.
Coffins and cabinets, their carpenter tools
Ciswen of the Forge bartered: *Unleavened,*
*good for long journeys,* she said with a laugh.
Woodworkers, she trained them to hammer nails.
Together they tended acorn and ash.
They relearned the art of stoneware, to grind
amaranth and ancient grains, time out of mind.

# GRANDMOTHER'S HIDDEN VALLEY LIFE

*As Told to Bramah by the Hidden Valley Makers*

By day Grandmother toiled in a factory.
Eyes downcast, joining with assembly lines.
Consortium-controlled farm labourers,
they saved apples marked "Modification."
Seeds plucked on their shift, dried on patched linen.
Commandeered scientists punched out their cards,
faster to the belt, Consortium-sealed.
Factory workers smiled, pickers for a meal.
Not one manager aware of their plot,
earth a means to rebel, to save seeds, stock.
Not one guard, deserting, to stumble in——
We though knew each pergola spell unlocked
afternoons without a whisper of wind.
Seeds peeled back to reveal species, husks ground
mortar to stone, powders mixed for healing,
butter paper and an old silver spoon.
Her hut, scavenged lumber cast-off plywood
tarps and cedar, seaweed and hot pitch,
> her methods proved true.
Roots entwined to form a watering dish,
cupped hole in the stony earth, prized by all—
> giant sakura bent from the Before,
> no blossoms, withered stems, and no birds sang.

Afternoon in Grandmother's hut we crept,
fragrant breads, kale stalks, barley soup, crushed thyme.
Grandmother tilled her plot of land: the names
fell from her fingertips, arnica, sorrel.
Afternoons in the far meadow she worked,
quotas established by the high command.

She refused their huge irrigation schemes.
She said no to their monoculture fields.
     She said *al-fasfasa* instead of *alfalfa*;
*sweet clover mix* instead of *cover cropping*.
     Barley and fava beans, pulses and peas,
          cereals and turnips, collard green stalks,
to grow, to harvest, to save, stooped to tend
leaf, flower and seed, fennel and hawthorn,
          secretly imported *ashwagandha*.
Outcast traders brought us shards of glass jars,
Consortium crumbled; refugees fled.
     All of us who'd escaped calamity:
daisy hearts to mullein, St. John's wort, weeds;
before the wind blew, we'd gather the seeds.
*Chop, grind and soak, find a dark place, then shake*
*macerate the menstruum, muslin cloths make.*
Beggar children sang these words. She fed them.
We learned again. Found traders, bartered for:
glass, alcohol, cloths, rakes and shovels, sticks—
we learned to make do, we learned wind and sun.
We captured snowmelt by digging deep ponds,
bruised leaves to wounds, tinctures sipped slow,
          in this way she helped us heal.

♛

### Grandmother's Recipe Book

She coaxed good things from herbs picked or dried,
water saved in stone pots, where she cleaned homes
inside Perimeter, gated, guarded.

Glass vials over wood fires, her method.
*Macerate, menstruum,* she'd whisper, working
bellows to flame, barterers, traders, thieves

welcomed: one hand at her waist, the other stirring
petals, stalks, leaves, oil, honey, fermented.
Lavender, basil, thyme, skullcap, Sweet Anne,

milk thistle, hops, and valerian, too.
Chop, grind, plants to powder, ethanol moist:
*Weeks to dry and weeks to soak,* she told us.

Stir to mix, keep all dark and shake each day.
She jotted down notes, weight-to-volume; saved
rolls of muslin cloth, jars of alcohol.

Coloured glass on cedar shelves, cool dark hut.
*Materia medica* her two books:
she called them *Avicenna* and *Al-Nabati.*

She told us: *Strain and press, count out your weeks.*
*Keep hot water close by, stir and let sit.*
*Use your nose and your tongue, always taste first!*

> *Facsimile Insert*
> Grandmother's *Avicenna,*
> made up of two torn scrolls,
> *Kitab Al-Shifa* also *The Quran*
> Venus to the sun, metals transmuted
> she'd clipped and saved her own cuttings, pasted
> bits and pieces, folklore and fact, her thoughts—
> collage of lived experience, hard times.

♛

*Seeds Saved (taped packets, inside cover)*

Peas      Beans
Tomatoes  Lettuce
Peppers

### Grandmother's Rose Garden

We'd climb the low Boundary wall, jump down
footfalls on dry soil, puffs of dust, snapped twigs.
Seventeen rose beds, petals glowing bright.
Honey Perfume floribunda; Fragrant
Plum grandiflora, smoky purple-edged.
Big golden yellow Radiant, citrus scent.
Soft pink Heritage, sweet lemon, cup-shaped.
Bourbons, cabbage blooms, hybrid tea, damask:
white-petal-packed orbs. Fragrant Clouds, coral—
repeat blooming, climbers, rich cherry-red edges
deepening with time, clip, snip, Grandmother's hands
secateurs pressed against old woody growth.
Deep raspberry, rich velvety, rugosa
       trailing, climbing, ruffled spirals
strong spicy sweet scents!

### Grandmother's Moon Songs

If by lavender, call her light, silver.
Cy-Board messages posted before loss.
Kitchen sill harvest, windows exploding—
if electronic, sos, then gold

pulses in our own morse code, sent frantic.
If by candlelight and under refuge
wash pods; save paper towel, last remnants.
Our fingers, tweezer extractions, tremble,
blot out the street sounds, gunfire to kernels.
Packets shaken in 3-D, then filmed slow.
Remember to show us each filament.
If by yarrow, saved from the Last Summer
allow yourself hot water tisane soothed—
Look up! *Blicket Auf!* Her face smiling runes.
We brought with us tucked in canvas sacking:
*Lobelia Kalmii,* chanting *unbranched.*
Did we forget to mention black nightshade
berries ripened to less harm, water gulped.
Spurious gifts from travelling mendicants.
Mountain valley trekkers, yellow head trails.
Sky bright, she held charts, Vega to the east:
hearth side, brown hands twining two sticks,
    fire god
       appeased.
Turmeric, cardamom cakes baked, soft rounds
shaped by deft fingers, roll, tuck, pull, snip, pat
floury soldiers, squat heads waiting heat.
Pink ladies, hard crunch, small mutations rubbed.
First light before dawn, needle to thumb, pressed
one droplet, staining her signature red,
one beeswax candle, and we to witness:
*Heartsick for you, Bramah,* her Portal calls.
Wordless urgings sent out with each star's light:
*Come back, Raphael's working in the dust.*
Douglas fir, spruce, western hemlock, cedar.
Grandmother one night told us to write down:

All our shrines the earth will swallow untouched.
Huge stone pillars unblemished, site names lost.
Only Bramah will be our wayfinder,
her ship will be called *The Great Year Forward.*
She'll take us there, she'll make things right, seasons
    will be restored one day, just you wait and see——

## BRAMAH INSIDE THE MAKERS' CIRCLE

Price Park, without her secret codes, barren.
To find the way in, we knew to sit still.
Awaiting the Makers' Circle under
the six oaks, or the huge Spanish chestnut.
Here we asserted the right to repair,
we figured out how things work, how to fix
tire rings and old Big E ration cards
with the stamps, transmitters with cables sourced.
We learned again to beat ploughshares, make soap,
our mantra not to throw: *To Patch and Mend.*
It were Bramah who first taught us—codes cracked,
Consortium's secret algorithms
stolen, deciphered, shared:
the right to repair carefully restored.

As stitched inside cloaks or etched on clay urns:
*We make our corners rounded.*
*We turn away from cold iron*
*sharp metal melted*
*wood chiselled, scraps saved.*

As heard on evenings when the Portal opened
just enough:
*How cool and sweet the air damp with living.*
Once temperate, air flows, currents, gulf streams,
moderated mechanisms intact;
now, extremes. Sudden and unpredictable.
We aim for comfort, our hands resist change,
each day of the Dry we long for the Wet,
we march under blue skies laughing at us
sun burning skin, earth's core shaking,

oracles sent, reminders. *The world not*
        *even about us,*
intoned Grandmother, cross-legged, encircled.
In the fading light of the afternoon
so sat the Makers and sang these small tunes.
Bramah's arrival marked by her soft cry,
        *I found you!*
In this way the locksmith met her people,
        no fond embrace, a circle of story:
our breath held, released, our gaze on Bramah
        entering within.

♛

# MY NAME IS MYRIAM

(handwritten in pencil, almost faded away)
brown hands trembling, she gave this to Bramah:

I always knew to keep my ways and means:
linden-banyan import, long-limbed and grafted
I spun my tales under lime-green branches,
all my chants to fool drone surveillance carts.
I learned to splice East to West, propagating
hybrids dipped in fertilizer, my own herbs.
In the base of each earthenware pot, stones,
flecks of gold, the tiniest garnets glowed.
Cuttings taken from tips and rooted, pinched.
I knew by sight, half-inch stem nodes,
pencil-thick brown wood, both ends,
manure from my own goats' ground,
cover droppings no one allowed to touch,
buckets, inside: thickness the length of a pencil.
Fingers on the pages of old books, stained,
yellowed, ripped, taped: each morsel baked, a sign,
all making is a gift from the divine.


Bramah took the faded paper and smiled.

# BRAMAH LISTENS AGAIN TO GRANDMOTHER

Settler and uninvited, I've seen things.
Save my words and remember for later:

## The Call to the Light of the Moon

Covert, we knew to empty our pockets,
lance-shaped leaves, two-lipped corolla stamens,
five-stalked, rubbed erect, acrid milky juice.
We warned against tomato, rhubarb leaves,
potato sprouts, apple seeds, cherry pits,
them grocery produce finds, from the Before.

Our heads turned upward on nights of no moon.
She would still be there we knew, if chanting,
*Baneberry, camas, hemlock, bittersweet.*
*Even if invisible your light shines out.*
Circled close, shoulder to shoulder, hands clasped.
*Bunches of scarlet, we'll not forget drought.*

♛

## The Call to the Seasons

The Weather Is the Deepest Portal of Them All.

Circling the dry well, we heard voices:
*The Last Rose of Summer, we all sang soft.*
*Abandoned farmhouse, swallows in the loft.*

Then Grandmother led us into her grove:
settler and uninvited, I've seen things;
save my words and gather seeds for shade.

## The Call to Thuja Plicata

Scaly blunt needles. Press pairs, tight to twig.
Limbs sweeping downward, tapered trunk, fluted base.
Spheres of female, small cones, separate from male.
Dead branches in the crown, dense foliage.
Long-lived, slow growing, these trees we called *The Watch*.
Settlers, we knew their magic not for us.
Our language schemed ways to label, to take.
Buds chewed for toothache, bark twigs, infused, steamed.
Boats, houses, shingle and shake; fence posts and rope
threads. Demarcation obsessed, we copied,
stole, long strips, separate layers, bark to wood.
Hauled water, boiled; sifted ash to soften
dried filaments, pounded along the grain.
Splinters pulled over ridges before rain.

Small breezes carrying, words echoing:
*Hollyhocks, daisies, snapdragons and peas—*
*these we once loved in the Hidden Valley.*

Cedar boughs underfoot, her knees earthbound.
Eyes closed, reciting, fingers on her thighs,
settler and uninvited, I've seen things.
Save my words for later when the wars come.

## The Foretelling

Honey-brown S-curves, undulating shape
Sonali the Golden, sly, beauty made
well before her sister, Abigail-ji
lost, hurled down the Portal of Wind and Rain.
*Sonali, Sonali*, father unknown.
When oak turns to russet, you'll find her here.
Honey-locust green shading to golden.
Sherronda, your mother, she'll outwit men.
*Sonali, Sonali*, father unknown.
When oak turns to russet, you'll find her here.
Settler and uninvited, I've seen things.
Save my words for later when the great ship arrives.

*Sonali and Sherronda*, names unknown.
We knew better than to ask.
We rubbed, and stored, and held.
Most of us forgot.

# GRANDMOTHER'S TALE OF THE LAST PORTAL

Ambling down the road, Death and Time, slack-jawed,
loose-limbed, slouching toward Perimeter.
Pale skin, shining, hours before the dawn.

Seated, then, on two square cut granite blocks,
elbows to knees, patient and observant.
*Everyone in the end always comes to us.*
Wordless message seeping into the rocks,
not a sliver of green or one soft thing
to melt their indifferent, implacable resolve.

Past the granite blocks, the old Wishing Well
long since empty, no buckets to be found.
Two Aunties in rags, fingers to lips,
pulled us aside and pointed the way round.
Fingers crossed, we stepped and made not a sound.

We didn't dare turn to look at the gate.
Veils, cloaks, scabbards, thrown off before the lake.
Them two Aunties, ragged, digging their soil,
resting their tools on those forever blocks——

*Now,* said Grandmother, *never mind this tale.*
She dropped into our hands one blue stone egg,
three packets of seeds, marigold and beans.

*Refuse tragedy,* she called out to us.
*I've seen the destruction of everything.*
*I've learned from Bramah to cleave to green—*
she raised her hands to woman workers, chained—
*so that our skin might be golden again.*

Words echoing against granite we walked
steps away from a green-painted oak door.
Grandmother's spells and seeds in our pockets.
Month's end, hidden portals leading to sound.
Snapdragons, buttercup fields whispered, *Seeds*—

# GRANDMOTHER AND THE SEED SAVERS SING TO BRAMAH

Abandoned concrete blocks, handfuls of soil.
Four Aunties with their backs to the wind, bend:
*Drought, famine, wars and plague, our seeds still saved.*
Their heads draped in scarves, limbs in folded rags.

Before dawn, Grandmother rose and walked miles,
hidden allotment camouflaged from drones.
She'd help them dig furrows, crumbled earth,
fingers tracing a series of letters,

all the words for water, stick end to stone.
Four Aunties and Grandmother to divine:
*No one else will come and we can't wait, now!*
For forty days and much longer, they prayed.

We heard a bard sing "The Before-Time Blues."
Generation on the cusp, no going back,
*Temperate to extreme from then on, only—*

Our homes as if matchsticks, struck, then folded.
Giant's hand down to wipe us from this earth,
banished from homes inside Perimeter,
regulated to Rentalsman, one room.

Grit filled furnace, the Dry, withering crops.
Berries bleached white, plums stunted, riverbeds
parched. Rain an absence, dreamt of for months, years.
She led us to the oak, five thousand rings,

old enough to transmit beyond memory.
Mythic, mapped, carved, the longest table known,
letters chiselled in a myriad of tongues,
spherical objects moving at great speed,
visible, true words of all believers:
*We'll come back—in twenty-five-nine-two-oh.*
*We'll come back—in twenty-five-nine-two-oh.*

## THE HUNT FOR THE YOUNG RAPHAEL

She taught us to turn our hands to the wind.
We stood with our backs to the lower breeze.
We looked to the clouds, coming down left, rain
hoped for and also dreaded, burning
where once was sustenance, now toxic fumes
stirred up ghosts, memories, longing.
Membrane between dimensions thinner,
psyche flooding layers of the past, un-
requited, unfinished, sighs and whispers.
Aunties fled from the Wishing Well gone dry.
*The Last Rose of Summer*, that portal gate,
another dimension, seldom found.
*One day we will take our leave of this place.*
Undertones of speech, snippets shared, slantwise.
*Oh forever and a day*, we sang soft.
October, as then was called, divining
the living and the dead, diaphanous
            dimensions thinner.
The Portal still able to send, release
chestnut trees and oak, Perimeter parks
outspreading, *Winter-spring-summer-fall*, the boys sang slow
no longer understanding what the words meant.
Swords home, battleworn, trailing their weapons:
*Every nook and cranny, find, fix and mend.*
*We know Sherronda was once Shanti-Ben.*
None of us knew what they meant, sideways chants.
Around their necks, medallions with numbers
25,920—gold filigree.

*Bramah*, cried Grandmother, *find that oak box!*
In the oak box, one Shiva calendar
magic Before-Time record of the past.

In the calendar you'll find a way in
what once were the months of the Lost Seasons.
Inside, portals, what once were weather.
Inside the weather, you'll find names, calling—
Inside the names, you'll find him,
green and golden, Raphael, dust covered.

## The Young Raphael & His Story

## AS RECORDED BY T-LOHK AND CIRCULATED BY SEED SAVERS

*Used to be Price Park*
*Used to be the Battle of Kingsway*
*Beware the Wet, Beware the Dry*

Came the times, and they were bad. We found him,
*Concreting the Future* on his T-shirt,
stencilled slogans, ripped cotton, muddy boots.

Mixer on wheels, slow to fast, not his truck,
indentured many times over, chain-ganged.
Oval turning concrete, labour for hire.

No matter which shift, his skill made him lead.
*I'm good with my hands,* he'd say with a laugh.
Every cast-off found a way to his shift.
Death symbols forbidden on their tattoos.
Raphael the leader, workers without masks,
unvaxxed, called at any moment to build
bigger and better, roads, towering malls.

*Used to be Price Park*
*Used to be the Battle of Kingsway*
*Beware the Wet, Beware the Dry*

No one left to hear snippets of his songs,
      heart full of remembrance
          his growing up
              orphaned and alone,
save for Grandmother who kept telling him,
      *Your mother and your father—*
            but Raphael refused to believe.

# RAPHAEL AND THE ALL-ALONE JINI

Once after lightning struck our linden tree,
great sheets split the mouse-grey sky: S-curved strikes——
Aunty Magda ran me underground.

Crystal cavern sunk near and neath our well,
Thunder shook the glimmery walls: I cried,
*Save us, Bramah,* and my Aunt laughed. Shuffling

in the dark, she soon lit beeswax candles
pure without smoke, flickering yellow flames,
my eyes large as saucers, sweet-scented air.
Aunty Magda rubbed her hands, stamped her feet:
before us in the dark, a woman danced——
my eyes wanted to stare but they closed tight.

Look now, two voices told me, and I did!
Seated cross-legged, a Jini who smiled
somehow, although I loved to chat, my lips

sealed as if with honey-wax, my words stopped.
Only now years later, I see again
her silver hair, brown skin and flashing eyes.

Tale after tale, squatting there with my aunt,
they forbade me to ever speak of this:
*Raphael,* my Aunty Magda said, *sit.*

*Behold the Jini of the All-Alone!*
She holds a thousand names of all who died
in sickness, afraid, not one soul to see,

not one hand of their own blood to hold fast.
Every year a thousand names even more
when moths flutter instead of bees, bare limbs,

cracked branches, ash caked on leaves, falling down.
This All-Alone Jini then turned her head:
her flashing eyes! Her silver hair in dreads.

*Raphael,* she said. *Raphael.*

Years later still, Raphael heard again
this story told by foot soldiers marching
west to east, before the fall of Baghdad.
Some of the Guards would laugh and shake their heads,
chins jerked toward the back, woman warrior
steps always receding, head silk-covered.
When Raphael asked about her, they said,
*Oh, that's T-LOHK: Best leave her All-Alone.*
Everyone laughed. He never spoke of it again.

# RAPHAEL GROWING UP

*Life in Rentalsman*
*as recounted by Raphael*
*from what his grandmother told him.*

We waited for the winds,
        we waited for the rains.
Chopped wood, picked up sticks,
        our bees stayed inside.

Mornings all we had to do was plug in.
Big E endless, paid for with a quick flick,
those generators and those dams, for us.

This were Before the Takeover when
life was simple, filled with choices, options:
everywhere reserve armies delivered.

Meals to eat, sofas, tables, all made cheap.
Mornings our kettles, sleek cords attached,
water in a faucet, those Plumbers' Guild

coupons came in handy if things broke down.
Our devices handheld, sold us each thing,
swipe and turn on: our push-button machines

sang to us, our tasks complete, we sat down.
Evenings to disappear, staring at screens.
Our cars slept well in their underground berths.

Instant access, we entered the Inside.
All our wires hidden; we knew to buy:
we needed so many things and clicked, swiped!

Imagine our world: select and apply.
No one to teach us—how things fall apart.
To read the blossoms, birdsong and stars.

# RAPHAEL AND THE AUNTIES

### Raphael Remembers Aunties in the Guild Halls

From the hands of one aunt to the other,
past all the Guild Halls: soap makers, weavers,
my eyes, round saucers, to see glass-blowers:

their row of Mason jars behind straw skeps,
beekeepers' candles, and at The Three Bakers:
ovens filled with rising half-crescent moons
that flaked in the mouth, melting with butter.

The best place: to sit at Ciswen's forge,
her two huge arms, her flaxen braids swept,
anvil and tongs, her stories of Bramah.

*Raphael,* Ciswen would laugh, *my angel*
*remember the weak, the better to help.*
And then her words breaking off in fire——

Those woodworkers with their lathes, sharp high sounds
piercing grey skies, toxic rain, concrete slabs
used to separate each stall, filled with things.

I'd grab broken bits of glass to make pipes,
slender beakers with which we watered plants,
tomatoes, beans and squash, Magda taught me

to save seeds, to gather, dry and store well.
*Never give up on living things,* she'd say,
our hands clipped curled leaves, white moths, fluttering——

Overhead crude carvings, cut letters read,
DOES GOD DEMAND DAY LABOUR? LIGHT DENIED.
If ever I said these words out loud, how my aunties
        laughed, cigar smoke curling from their lips.

Then they'd cough and exclaim,
        *Patch and Mend!*

### Raphael Remembers Aunty Magda, the River Dweller

*When I was a young boy*, said Raphael,
*my Aunty Tabitha brought me to her.*
*Magda, by the Goodbye River, we said,*
        *teach us a turn, splice us a tied-knot rope—*
Days, I'd run to her hut by those damp banks.
*Mind you never fall in;* she'd laugh and twist,
sisal and twine, we'd stretch the yarn she'd spun
under and over, three twists of fibre:

fibre into yarn
yarn into strands
twist this way then turn

stretch the rope
begone kinks
whip these ends.

Magda sat for hours, chanting to twist.
My fingers bled red, my neck cramped to learn:
*Give us a smoke and we'll pull your frayed rope.*
Her teeth still strong in her old face, she'd laugh.
She'd spit tobacco then pause and look straight
past me into the blank black box ahead,
                unplugged from anything, dust-covered shelf.

## Raphael Remembers Aunty Magda's Teachings

She baked us honey cakes to soothe bad dreams:
hives stacked in two tiers on a ledge of rock,
brushwood covered a base of stone——two poles.
She made us, boys and girls, to sweep and clean.
*Get your hearth ready every morning. Sweep!*
Each dawn get up early and offer space——
that Lady Luck might alight your mantel.
And don't you dare call on Bramah too quick:
she come only when you choose another.
Then Magda coughed and turned and looked at me.
*Raphael, Raphael,* she would say soft
enough for the two of us to nod and wink.
Swords would tease me and Beggars make fun,
story to story, these unbroken links.

## Raphael Remembers the Disappearing Box

I can still smell the mud from the river
crows and sandpipers fought for scraps of meat
inside her hut, those dust-covered screen squares
portable devices, flat screen mounted
gone forever, the Big E unlimited
wireless controlled by Consortium.
I'd tap on the blank screens and close my eyes
in those days dust rained down on us, toxic:
we was always wiping those blank flat screens.
I wanted to run up to the Wishing Well
get far far away from all them doomsayers.
Magda would say, *Don't be a nincompoop.
Why don't you barter for a Big E pass?*
I did that and we got a few hours.

Years later those flat screens led me to her.
Hologram plates plugged in; recorder fixed.
My mother's voice, the colour of her hair.
      On screen, an old oak box, smooth lid, opening——
Inside the old oak box, an instrument
likes of which I'd not seen, glass slides, knobs turned
upright, black, spinning in 3-D without instruction.
Somewhere inside of me whispered words echoing,
*Chalice*, yet I didn't know the word, only
something——faint emanation, *Jump the Fence* ...
Cobweb memories I shook away, set foot
again on the path, knowing without knowing
*Bartholomew*, a word to find, a man;
*Bramah*, locksmith to open the oak box.
Outside, Beggars and Swords sang,
      *Sweeping wet streets,*
            *longing for seasons, cycles complete.*
      Bramah on the search for Raphael
            and the boy with the gap-toothed grin.

♛

### Raphael's Encounter with the Beggar Boy

After the Battle of the Bitter Green,
after honey hunting in the wild oaks,
after catalpa, cedar, gates and doors,
he'd tumbled clear of the Guards, stacked portals,
gap-toothed grin disappearing, battered shoes,
lost; finding his way by stars and by spells.
*Bramah*, he'd call, left shoulder raised windward.
All his energy gathered to summon.
Heart aching he pressed onward; head downcast.
His gaze followed the line: cracked gate, unhinged,
creaking back and forth, red, yellow, brown, black
rusted iron, steel, crumbled to his touch,
one arm toward the gate, he stepped forward—

Dropped in an instant: Perimeter's edge,
the world as he knew it, yet different.
Ahead on a dusty path a young boy
who turned at the sound of lopsided steps.
Years later some would recall this meeting:
    *Brothers, cousins, somehow connected, sure.*
Now, long lines of migrants trudged to the bridge.
The Beggar Boy followed his new friend, though.
Both boys turned away from checkpoint entries.
Both stole glances at each other and walked
past bus stops, down a highway ditch, ridged hills.
Supply trucks roared through the stink of diesel.

*Come meet my Aunty Magda, come and meet Grandmother.*
*Huh,* said the Beggar Boy, *guess I'll tag along.*
Both boys stood inside the Hidden Valley.

No vows of friendship were exchanged, and yet.

♛

### Sneaking Inside Perimeter's Archive with Aunty Magda

*Her purpose clear,* said the man
at the desk, by then the library.
*It were to rewrite the history*
*of the times and so her intent—*
And with that they bustled them out—
Raphael, the Beggar Boy and their books.
Grandmother waited outside, smoking and coughing.
They all boarded the bus after hours standing in line.
Seated, Grandmother and Aunty Magda kept smoking.
The bus driver turned on the Big Voice speakers:
NO SMOKING ON THIS BUS.
Grandmother and Aunty Magda laughed and coughed.
They told the boys these tales.
Everyone on the bus craned closer to listen.

♛

### The Tale of the Blasted Oak Box

*Set about finding,* she told her brood
from Tower Juniper.
*Names to hunger for,*
*to delight—*

### The Tale of the Fisherman's Knot

Grandmother taught Raphael who taught other children
fingers to keep the short ends five times big:
length to diameter, rope scavenged, kept
two sliding overhand knots
under-under, under-over, pull-pull,
knots to kiss, tighten to complete
and pull-pull, young hands tugged.

### The Tale of the Last Brigade

The child called Raphael
bent over the ripped packaging.
How he had come to know secret codes, chants
       no one could say.
*Assam*, he whispered. *Darjeeling.*
*Dark red*, said a girl, name un/known.
*Green China tips, Yorkshire blend.*
The children spoke together.

*I love this story*, said Raphael.

Grandmother smiled.

As soon as this story finished, the bus lurched to a halt.
PRICE STREET PARK blared the Big Voice speakers.
Grandmother and Aunty Magda exchanged smiles.
Under their breath they said, *Hidden Valley to us, Mrs. Bus.*
Said Aunty Magda to Raphael, *Find your father.*
Said Raphael to the bus passengers, *East wind riders.*
Said Aunty Magda to both children, *Smear mud on your face.*

Said the Beggar Boy, *I dreamt once of Bramah's golden key.*
Masks slipping off their noses, Grandma and Aunty Magda
grabbed the boys. Everyone tumbled out onto Boundary.
In no time at all, not one truck roaring past saw any of them.

## THE ADVENTURES OF THE YOUNG RAPHAEL
## AND THE BEGGAR BOY

Days later, on the road, on the run, hiding out, brothers in arms,
the Beggar Boy told Raphael,

*One day I shall tell you my real name.*
*Today, I must leave you.*

*First, though, pay attention:*

### Raphael Listens to the Beggar Boy's Story

And with the key I found that old oak box.
And in the box, her black instrument, glass
slides to insert, knobs to turn, eyepiece fittings,
*chalice,* a word from some memory deep inside,
plus a map and on that map
      stained blood-red, ripped parchment,
          the letter *A.*
I tore the seal, I read her words, and then——

Raphael, no longer kneeling to hear
cried, *we have to call Bramah back to us!*
Head raised, staring straight toward the misty hills,
low cloud overhanging, a name on the wind.
And the Beggar Boy laughed, not knowing his own end.

Together the boys ran to the old Wishing Well.

*I tell you; I tell you,*
*from Tower Juniper, not a sound,*

*not from Tower Oak*

*not from Tower Pine*
*neither Fir nor Ash,*
*and not a sound*

All the women there bent close to the rim,
where deep down the "I Tell You" song echoed.
All the women there washing and cleaning

*auguries transported, I tell you, I tell you*
*not a sound, not a person seeing anything*
*only Beggars and Swords sweeping dust, leaves.*
*Upright, they sharpen, weapons to shoulders*
*all roads lead to Paris, parched throats and dry——*

Raphael shrugged his shoulders and grinning said,
        *All this doom and gloom!*
        *Let's go hunting for the Lost Portal.*

♛

## THE FURTHER ADVENTURES OF RAPHAEL
## AND THE BEGGAR BOY

*You'll have to find Bramah,*
          said the Beggar Boy, his shoelaces always in a knot.
*No,* said Raphael, *she'll have to find us!*
Year's midnight fading to grey skies and snow.
*To the Four Seasons, all cycles complete,* sang Raphael.
Portal tumblers, fast friends,
          they jumped to bridge Times Past.
At the Gate of the Lost Seasons, they kicked at stones.
Chalice and oak box, science and craft, they knew.
          *For ever and a day, I'll meet you here.*
Almost a smile, not quite, the Beggar Boy
cleared his jump, one-handed salute, deep blue.
He'd given Raphael a map and key, which Raphael lost!

Little did they know that Bramah searched too.
Gold locket at her neck, waiting and true.
Bramah knew how to tumble a portal.
          Raphael thought he knew.
Bramah's portal jumps revealed:
the place Pacifica, drought to the Wet
the time the future, forward and back
the past alongside the present—locks turned
          doors with a single keyhole
                    only Bramah's hands to work
          gold pass carved on its side, runes, shimmering
                    red and turquoise, past the door, a wall
                    behind the wall, secret gardens
                              beyond oak and banyan
                                        libraries, war camps

once Alexandria, once Constantinople
Pacifica to Baghdad
long-forgotten books, scrolls, tablets
old computers left to die, hoarded
semi-conductors. Of all these,
neither child knew or saw a thing.

♛

*Jump the Fence*, the beggar children urged.
And so, they did. Alas, the Beggar Boy captured by a rogue portal.
Raphael yelled for help, *Bramah!*
No one came, of course.
Raphael caught sideways in a gulley.
Every time he tried to climb out,
water to water, unrelenting.
He wandered for the night.
Dawn broke torrential, railway beds washed out,
roofs sagged, gulls calling, the weight of water.
Ah, the Wet replaced the Dry and Raphael cursed.
The Beggar Boy disappeared.
Raphael trudged back alone to Grandmother and the Hidden Valley.

Unbeknownst to Raphael, this also happened:

Deep one moonless night, by the six oaks,

Grandmother, heart heavy, called forth visions.

♛

## Grandmother's Vision Locates the Lost Beggar Boy

Grandmother bent low
  her lips murmured to the trees
*eternal chess board, climate change, checkmate*
  *Bramah, come to us, your boy is at the gate.*
Said the Beggar Boy, soft, to Grandmother:
  *I've got these pieces, see, unravel my cloak.*
  *Chalice to find, smoke-heart to see,* these words
arrow to the soul, not even a whisp of wind, not even the faintest emanation.
Grandmother's jaw set in a firm line.
She leant back against one of the oak trees. She closed her eyes.
  Above her, unseen, one barred owl flew.
   Grandmother opened her eyes.
   There, on the ground, an image:
   heart of the courtyard, Royal Baghdad.
   The Beggar Boy seated, cross-legged
    small brown hands on chess pieces.
   Doomed to play with Al-Rashid.
   Each move to last a century's combat
    ground ozone, knight takes bishop, save the queen,
    East Antarctic Ice Sheet, protected pass.
Now, intense emanations travelled far distances.
Grandmother stood up. She heard words clear as a bell.
  The barred owl hooted once.

*Through the Portal of the Lost Seasons, no choice but to jump!*
Grandmother sighed, looked over her shoulder at the still sleeping camp.
She held her vision to herself. She repeated, *Strix varia, be wise.*
At dawn, her bones stiff with cold, each silent breath calling for Bramah
  to arrive.

When Raphael woke, his neck sore against the bark of the tree,
not one sign left of the Beggar Boy.
He pestered Aunty Magda all morning.
He whined and whinged at Grandmother, who just laughed and coughed
as she packed up their things.
*Jumped the Fence*, she called out, lifting her hands to the breeze.

♛

And so, the years, whiplashed: drought to flooding,
        heavy, unceasing, everything sank.
*Thirty days*, we sang outside The Last Gate of the Four Seasons.
Used to be we could count on four, now two:
the Dry and the Wet, and *Oh when she blows*
deluge to soak, crumble, overflow, falling,
soils weak, tree roots bare, once scorched in the Dry.
Outside, children roamed singing, *Thirty*
*Hath September, Just Like November.*
        Not many left to explain to them
                what the words meant.
If scorched, then soaked, months collapsed,
Hidden Valley life, patch to mend, repaired,
        we carried on.
As for Raphael, he grew restless,
        believing in little, save the need to survive.
Round the campfire, called *If Only*. He'd turn away
        from any stories of *The Beggar Boy*,
                and sat silent, staring into flames.
And so, the years, whiplashed: drought to flooding,
        heavy, unceasing, everything sinking
                no way to predict the future
                        lost seasons—Raphael
                                just shrugged his shoulders.
He found work, got drunk (a lot) and kept going.

# RAPHAEL IMPRISONED

*As recounted by a sympathetic Tribunal executive.*
*Inscribed by the Itinerant Scribe T-LOHK,*
*on contract to Consortium.*

We met that young man living porch-side, mercy
who worked, those people, foragers. It were
inside Rentalsman, after the first Catastrophe,
boy, insisting: to gaze in love prefigures
honey locust, angel mushrooms, all his finds
dew surrounded, tender orchard trees, pear-gold
apple, enough gaze to kill, asking *why,*
he thought: my love is strong enough to stand
longing, one look filled, enough to wither
jealous rain who takes the wind away, drenched
other places unseen and we, in drought.
And then that young man, known as Raphael
      cried: *I loved the honey locust and it died*
*the pear and apple tree, too.*

His cracked lips, his bruised skin, after silence,
despondent, his palms turned upward, lifelines cut
*Help me, I want to be free*—shadows

obligatory, the tribunal decreed:
Mind how you breathe when you work in the dust.
*And said, after seven years, you'll see.*

## CONSORTIUM CONCRETE

*Warning If You Are Experiencing—*

Before-Time brick wall grafitti-stencilled.

Conscript to sand, water, gravel, cement.
Make the slurry, build the bridges and dams.

All our towers, our parking garages,
carbon emissions in millions of yards.

Before our Fifth Catastrophe, towers
built to last, our cities, our fortresses—

Little did we know and then when we did
pouring and mixing, building our growth still

dioxide to ozone, limestone, and clay
thin layer sphere, we thought, *Impregnable.*

Mixing and heating those blistering slags.
Our Portland Cement, our steel and fly ash

coal and liquid gas, cars, and airplanes, fast
the years, our decline, glass crushed to powder

*Pozzolan,* we said, *and Carbon Cures, too.*
We tried shooting liquid into concrete

*Green,* we called it, and hopeful, we tried things.
We were wrong.

♛

## RAPHAEL THE CONQUEROR, AS SUNG BY SWORDS

We found him in Consortium Concrete.
Sad-eyed, loquacious, dusty and strong-armed.

He worked the night shift, and those Swords did tease:
*Hey Rafe, keep talking you'll never beat us,*

bed to lips, your warm stories, our cold hands
anyways, your mouth always moving; strange

orange flickers in rusted cans, your tales!
*Hey Rafe, sharpen your point, jab us again,*

laughing and lethal, they danced as he spoke.
Let it be said that he never won once—

Many a Sword who tried to teach him joust,
many an old woman who loved his words.

Wolves howled on the battlefield when he fell—
See him here before you, his songs to tell.

\*


Whenever he heard this song at day's end,
Raphael just shrugged his shoulders and laughed.

## RAPHAEL OVERHEARS TALES OF CONSORTIUM'S NEW GENERAL

One night in a tavern at the edge of Perimeter,
T-LOHK the Itinerant Scribe and a travelling troubadour
    shared stories of a new warrior general
    fighting battles in the east:

Her hammer engravings, tarnished, blacked-out.
Her soldier's cloak, cut in half and shared with—
Her cavalry horse, her mother's estate,
her own Shillong-Ashram where later parchments held:
hundreds of scribes, illuminated scrolls.
Consortium embellished all her stories.

Migrants to invoke the name Sherronda,
all the Guards of the Fifth Gate to recite:
(without a trace of irony)
*Be brave, help the poor,*
*share your things, fight hard.*
*Duty and orders: look up!*

Some said the truth, others swore
they knew what really happened.
Her invincibility either a myth or
propaganda. Sherronda on hire to Consortium.
They found her skills useful.

*Consortium edicts will never say*
*what wool weavers and innkeepers will tell.*
Sherronda the General said this with a rueful smile.
Outside Perimeter, sweeper boys sang:
      *Step right, keep tight,*
          *never miss your chance,*

*un coup de dés, jamais, jamais.*
Said Sherronda the Warrior General:
*Consortium told me to amputate*
*each arm of each boy who dared say*
*my real name, given to me at birth.*
Said T-LOHK to the troubadour: *Surely not?*
Said the troubadour, now well-soaked with drink:
*I pretended not to hear this.*
On the east wind I could hear the trees sing
    *Bramah! Come talk sense to this Shanti-Ben.*

When I woke, hungover and dry-mouthed, I vowed to erase this tale.
And never spoke of it. Until today. *Here*, said T-LOHK, *I'll buy you*
    *another round.*
The troubadour continued; words slurred.
T-LOHK the Itinerant Scribe listened.
So did Raphael.

Said Sherronda to her Honour Guard:
*Take these beggars to the Fifth Gate,*
*no questions asked.*
They did as told, with many sideways looks.
Said Sherronda:
*Always pay attention to sweepers.*
These were her words when she freed
    a young boy, gap-toothed grin.
There they stood at the foot of Shillong Peak.
In her hands a parchment scroll,
a small sack of chestnuts, a flask of wine.
Then she walked back to the city,
    burnt down the town hall,
    demolished the hospital.
*Enemy aliens*, she claimed.

Consortium approved.

Beggars tugged on Sherronda's coat,

*Un coup de dés, jamais, jamais.*

# RAPHAEL ALLOWED SIDE WORK AS A PRAISE SINGER

"He Sang of Lost Lovers"
Their tears would be a flood
against the gates of the world.
"He Sang of the Famished"
They'd write lines, verses to eat,
dawn's meagre feast—incarcerated.
"He Sang of Textile Workers, Freed"
They'd squat to trade and barter soft cotton.
"He Sang of Children Chain-Ganged into Trade"
Their haunches.
Their haunches covered with blue welts, then sold.
"He Sang of Mothers, Outraged, Still Indentured."
They'd do anything for a crust of bread.
"He Sang of Seed Savers Tortured for Belief."
Migrants and Makers would ask him slantwise:
*How do you know all these songs, where you from?*
Raphael would just smile and shake his head.

On a night of no moon, outside an inn
three beggar boys told him: your hands will heal.
By then, filled with wine, Raphael nodded,
almost asleep, he heard those boys whisper:

> *Remember the Fisherman's Knot.*
> *You'll find a daughter there!*

The next morning, miles along the East Road,
his cloak pulled close, his steps slow, wondering——

# FAREWELL TO GRANDMOTHER, BRAMAH FINDS RAPHAEL

*All things pointed to one direction home.*
This statement debated, guild hall to camp:
convergent and ordained or random chance.

Our seasons tilted, then change run amok.
Consortium control winnowed away.
Seed Savers led many uprisings.

Guards of the Fifth Gate deserted in droves.
Grandmother's messages sewn in our sleeves.
Evading Perimeter, we learned trades:

Patch 'n Mend brigades taught us to survive.

We learned to make stools and chairs from gleanings:
elm, ash, maple, beech, pine and sycamore,
planed by shared lathe or whittled with a knife.

Beggar children sent to fetch river sand,
their small hands to scrub or pack in clay.
Horizontal surfaces proved useful:

table to keep away pests, to cut food.
A stool to protect from damp earthen floors.
Lower the better to sit by hearth flames.

Smoke billowed, an owl hooted twice.

When Bramah arrived, we gave her the chair.
Everyone ducked away from the peat smoke.
By the fire sat Grandmother, twisting rope.

*You'll find him at dusk, splattered with concrete.*
Grandmother laughed and Bramah shook her head.
*First things first,* she said, and helped us pull twine.

## BRAMAH FREES RAPHAEL FROM CONCRETE CONSCRIPTION

Seen at dusk, quarry's edge, illicit garden
although he could be anywhere—
        clouds, the firmament of sky, his sometimes home,
a mud shack down by the river; or in the drop of a pit deeper
than any plot dug around here,
here is where I see him,
between noontime's sweat-drenched hours,
midday bisected by where he stands
at the foot of the eastern lot,
past a post of timber dug into the hardpacked clay,
tilted row of posts, boundaries to demarcate ours and theirs,
fitted tight with rocks. His feet in jackboot brown,
two days of stubble, coarser than sea salt, speckles his chin—
for all the dust of his clothing, no rents or rips serrate his knees,
the hem of his shirt, one side untucked, not unravelled.
His gaze steady but not on me, on the growth bustling
        around his feet:
        a blue hussy hydrangea,
        tomatoes sweet with yellow, quite wanton.
No aura surrounds my head—
why would it, I'm a stranger, my leather satchel thrown across one shoulder
and this young man in front of me, tall, restless,
        a tramp, a peddler, foot soldier, even town drunk,
although in this century, in this city, such descriptions wither, and look:
        white teeth against a brown smile, welcoming,
his black curly hair dusted with concrete.

♕

When he bends to strike a match against the edge of his heel—
　　　nothing about that foot suggests a limp,
visible only when he moves away,
up-down, up-down, that rhythm showing itself in steps.
The limp from day labour, making cement.

Can it be that the bright midday light accentuates the smell of him—
dried urine, sweat, a trace of fecal matter,
mixed humming scents of a bumper crop:
zucchini, squash still small for noticing—
all these ingredients distilled into a substance, inhaled,
escaping the reach of words, of the ghost of his long-dead mother.

It cannot be—that when his boot crushes a spent orange-capped needle,
(overhead the skytrain roars, the glass splinters)
the soil is seeded with anything but vitreous.
How my heart aches to see on his arm the place of the needle,
tiny green pinpricks to shoot down memory,
　　　young man with a habit and a limp, once golden,
　　　　　the aura of his parents so faint,
to speak their names defiles memory——
　　　rank days at the tavern, after long dusty shifts,
some other ineffable smell—
(quickly assumed to be just what it is:
a dog or man pissing for the hundredth time against that timber post).
　　　I shall intervene although forbidden!
Secret garden resting under drumbeats of rain,
let there be no heel marks from the man, no imprints,
snow-beaten, sun-evaporated, no sign of anything,
no one to exclaim at the place of the needle,
when, as in days of old, in the Before,
　　　where once in early September, runner beans would spiral

dozens and dozens, their long tendrils winding
across stakes driven into the clay-hardened ground,
let this man before me be once again green and golden.
Days from now we'll meet here again.
He'll tell me one evening when he bends to pluck the flower of the bean
(trim waist, strong thighs, marked arms, the place of the needle),
*Ah, this scarlet,* he will whack flower and leaf against those thighs,
*this scarlet, how she bites and burns—*
And we will set out, the two of us, on our journey.

♛ ♛ ♛
>>>>>>

## BRAMAH TELLS RAPHAEL THE WORDS OF THE ORACLE

That he would be made to travel afar
That he would be forced to rescue soldiers
That he must fight a battle not his own
That he should see a star and lose his voice
That he should heal himself and see again
That he should rescue a child and call her—

At this point Raphael interrupted,
  *Don't jinx me, Bramah!*

♛

## WHAT BRAMAH AND THE ORACLE FORGOT

They forgot to tell Raphael about the other lover.
They forgot to tell Raphael to count the number of moons.
They forgot to warn Raphael about his love, her flashing eyes!

They tried to do this later every night;
circled back to enter the realm of sleep
three taps, foreheads smoothed, cool-fingered pressure—

Machinations, gears interlocking tight
malevolent wheels clicked into their place
turn, grind, levers pulled the fate of others
luck battled chance, a thousand micro points:

decisions strung along a pulley-wire
time and its dimensions, portal mischief—
prick, ping, snap, cry—havoc—extend, release
Bramah forbidden to intervene, watched.

From down the long valley, from mountaintops
another thing they all forgot, Sword Girls
singing warnings, faint echoes through far lands:
*Every nook and cranny, find, fix and mend.*
*We know Sherronda was once Shanti-Ben.*
At the sound of the name, Raphael stood.
Neither he nor Bramah said anything.

*All Roads Lead to Paris: The Search for Bartholomew*

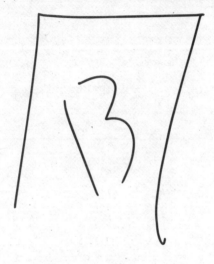

# IN THE DUNGEONS OF CONSORTIUM

*As Sung for Bramah by the Transport Prisoners*

Sing to us again of the Great Dying,
seashells engraved; driftwood inscribed, sand, clay—
Gather tusks, trilobites, rubbed ringed edges.

North, south, east, west—each wind sighs her tale
washed down to the depths that we might faint call—
never-ending hungers, consumers all:

*Mother of the Forest, branched to be brave*
*gather acorns, sticks and leaves, rubbed to burn*
*your roots embrace us, your rough bark makes us:*

*spinning and tilted, spheres, circles counted*
*sweet golden and green, always to be seen*
*burn us, make us, ringed edges, endless fall ——*

Belly full of worry, full of the sads;
crust of bread, a little drink, all the bads:
Beggars and Swords, with sabers and with pens,
joined forces with In-Betweens, they and them
banded together, their echoing songs.

Once temperate forests roared, scorched fiery,
our messages burnt crisp to ash, delayed,
who will be left to heed or to believe?

And Bramah said, *Tell me how to find Bartholomew.*
*First thing,* they said, *find the Scribe T-LOHK.*
And she did.

## AS RECOUNTED, BRAMAH & THE TRAVEL TALES

*T-LOHK, Itinerant Scribe Recounts a Series of Tales*

*Travel Tale #1*
Dublin. Of the Trade descended:
Ahmad Ibn Fadhlan, 921.
They said he'd lived centuries, portal to portal,
east to west and back again, scholars and fighters,
traders rendered by Consortium brought me news—
the Age, how to survive, how to fight drought,
divine water, seek the Eternal Game of Chess,
Ahmad Ibn Fadhlan, 921.
That long-ago portal traveller
said to have seen a beggar boy playing
in the Baghdad Court of Al-Rashid.

—walking, past the Customs House Quay
River Liffey, those bronze bodies, upright.
Thin, bent—this set down, I wrote one hundred

letters at the Cobalt Café, my words in ten
before thunder, an afternoon inside
humid, grit trolled under thumb, *O the Sea*
remembering famine, remembering the hoarded
grain stagnant, supply lines cut off
forest fires raging, no respite then from floods.
I studied all of these.

At the far end of the outside garden
unpatrolled, a man hid behind a newspaper.
He muttered, *The last word of a perfect language*
*Le dernier mot d'une langue parfaite.*

Seed Savers from Ballydehob, covert.
I kept them skep-safe in a grotto
against the wind, the hills roiled Atlantic
always turning to find, that farm long gone
Consortium approved, windmills to capture
        a sun's burning rays.
Energy the ultimate export.
Everyone wanting everything to stay the same.
The Seed Savers told me of a warrior in the east.
        Said her name was Shanti-Ben.
                Sister of Peace.

*Travel Tale #2*
Upstairs, Joyce House
I found a black leather notebook:

tracing fragments
parchment scraps

*ruin is contemplation*
*ruin is allegory*
*this city compound*
*beware the hunger*

*first the farmers then the soil.*
      Midnight and Guards drag small children, arms bent.
      Colonial where language is
      emulsified, images once teletyped
      bloodstream, messianic, the worst filled
            with words, the best without,
            the future a black box
      oak is possibility, shade will be the most prized
            commodity.

      Seed Savers escaped world over.
      Paris to Ahmedabad.
      Baghdad to Dublin.
      Pacifica transport planes
            flying low over the Irish Sea.
      Migrants in boats, shunted.
      The River Liffey.
            Customs House Quay.

Sun struck at that moment
unusual, and on these notes
wending, lines of refugees, migrants
    free trade textile workers
released and awaiting transport planes.
New systems of immigration, displacement.
Remains across the way of
sculpted figures, light on bronzed limbs
    those who longed to cross water.
*I took out their names,* written in lines
    accompanied by maps of aqueducts and old factories
where once things were made.

*Travel Tale #3*
*Sent far and wide by Consortium's scribes*
  *I walked Dublin*


Memory is a compound, transport planes, stalled.
News circulated among contractors
    Warrior General so full of story.
*Her flashing eyes, her floating hair!*
Followers amassed, chanting her exploits,
    claiming descent from an ancient trader,
*Ahmad Ibn Fadlan*, in the year 921.
    Along the Liffey at midnight, fragments:
past, present, future, the source, a river in the desert
written, spoken, forsaken, a river
    another courtyard, another memory,
        encircled—
light over my shoulder, tide washed, wind blown
saga to raga, exiled—outside Perimeter—
Those spires outside Hotel Ormond,
a musical fugue, reappearing, that cunning, to count
ten, and thunder, one hundred letters sent before the last—
It were a Thursday at the Cobalt Café, Dublin,
a table set for one
a place close to the window
a view to the back garden
a family holding, names not spoken.
See here, now, there's a man in the far corner
    his feet in brogues
    his face hidden by a newspaper
held upright—no one pays him attention.
There's the owner, long grey hair, pug-nosed,
round eyes. There's the woman and a woman younger, both heads
    dyed the same shade of bottle-red.

There's the well-heeled clientele, although
      North Dublin after drought and plague.
There's the width of the windowsill, a can of Illy syrup,
      silver tin, prop to hold,
air hot, humid, the merest wisp of breeze,
front dining, there's the cabinet with jewelry—
heirloom, *enquire at desk*, there's that garden out back, corridor to get through.
      Greek, Roman busts, on the way to the loo.
There's him now, coming to speak with me.
Something about a boy named Raphael.
Something about a man named Bartholomew.

# BARTHOLOMEW ON HIRE TO CONSORTIUM

*Inside 2 Square Adanson, 75005*
*As transmitted to Cy-Board #6*

I am upstairs this small apartment
Seed Savers' Co-op, Carcassonne.

Translations by the Hidden Valley Guild.
Famous unpublished treatise: *On Life Under Surveillance.*

Extolling the keeping, the finding
secret times for approaches to the moon.

How their smiles deepened
each time she refused an invitation

before midnight, before dawn
      at two in the afternoon

the garden, at the gate under shade
hot sun, nobody's business, and sideways.

*Glances contain everything,* they would say.
We were speaking of a secret book—

the book before the book, we shared Before.
Our world shattered, everything disappeared.

Untravelled, the ones that remained whispered
*obscura, camouflage, suggestions—*

hints, asides, the half-phrase, embedded design.
A love of tracing. Inside the covers, between the sheets—

Necessity: a small circle, not to say too much.
Codes, a means. Numbers. Lists.

These days, would never. Boulevards once green,
sandpits, stepped on, crumpled pieces, paper

all the baseless assumptions, not a whisper
voyeur, idle with tales, one should want

to be a spy on one's own life.
They said, *Yes, everyone needs a secret book*

*to be written in the garden, found inside*
*Perimeter.* Let field research be a requirement.

Month's end, moon's rise, a midnight train,
copy left on the seat behind the dining car—

afternoon in the archive, room with no view.
A record of events, these the Guild also translated.

And now, here in this safehouse, dare I write, too—

        tales of a praise singer.
His hair is red, his eyes are blue.
Some say he works for Consortium Concrete
        covered in dust and loquacious, tall, strong.
Some claim he is a spy of the Fifth Guard
        directed to trail me on orders of
                Consortium's star warrior general.
These names come to me in packets, tucked, hidden in seams:
        Sherronda, Raphael and the locksmith—
Seed Saver warnings, street corner glances
        they extolled the benefits of hiding in plain view.

♛

Everyone needs a secret book.
Something more dangerous than
*Dear diary*, found out, exposed—
I'm on hire to find word of an old oak box
        pieces of a chalice.
That was the price of my release.
To betray the mother of my child, lost son—
        night memories and the moon, my companions.

In this room, once prized by the INVESTIGATOR:
the floor a tableau, setting documented
once were two lovers, intent on escape—
rhythm, focus, hands to paper, thirty years old.
The still stink of old newsprint
loss, a collect of headlines
and then to sit back, haunches close to tile.
*Abigail, your absence my dreams do trace—*

♛

Days I work as directed, on contract.
Nights I surface desire, an urge, a calling
vocation, gift. Curse: to speak the names, naming—
and Mistress Fear, whose fingers clamp the gut
Hidden Valley Guild members implore
        to join the Resistance; and I, shirking, aware
        risk to be a bearer, all those tidings.
Outside, driven, to stand
up for what? At what cost—
Seed Savers asked, *Do you believe in ghosts?*
*Yes*, I answered. *Yes.*
And they asked, *Who is it who walks beside you?*

After months of no rain, sky-mouthing:
*Look for signs.*

♛

Ghost: my long disappeared love, Abigail, returns.
Chorus: *Je me souviens.*
Each night migrant woman workers roam the street.
Beggars and Swords sing: *Un coup de dés, jamais, jamais.*
Memory is sound relayed, impending
      imprisonment.
      *Fare Forward!* Oh Abigail.
And they cried to her, as taken, beaten, put out
      long lines stretched around Perimeter
            long lines now, all the rest of us.
Unwanted, we look for rescue waiting for Bramah.
Manacled, still able to call, *Jamais, jamais!*

♛

Moon up, gate opened, courts empty.
This very night, under no circumstance(s)
in the year of the reign, from Rentalsman
transported here, Paris, every city in ruins
to walk Perimeter—*let all evil die*—
Consortium has me, a bought man, for now.

## SMUGGLED IN FROM A CARAVANSERAI

*Torn from Bartholomew's notebook, found by T-LOHK,
given to Bramah, who reads as Raphael looks over her shoulder*

In the year of the reign 2104
I, Bartholomew, man of many journeys
——witness to experiments, on seeds and on humans
    interrogations, Resistance fighters, migrants from rogue portals
    having foretold the coming of the Fifth Catastrophe
    having marched into shadow, ombre——three-carded fate
    hands shaking, stitched seeds, riches to rags
    yearning for shade in the desert, resistant to orders
    unforsaken, slaked; having written, *scead(u)we, sceadu*
    inscribed, hidden, shielded. The dark——in prison, released
    my skills found necessary. Consortium logistics
    supply-side economics, trickle-down wages
    austerity and cuts, trying anything to keep the new normal.
    Out of prison, on contract, these Guards tell me
    *Consortium outsourced all our wages.*
    They tell me how lucky I am: useful with inscription codes,
    pens hoarded by the Prefect of the Fifth Gate.
    *Beware the warriors of the east,* chanted streetside, Beggars & Swords.
        *Brutal intent to cleanse, they'll follow the strong*
        *no mercy for the weak, they'll turn on a dime.*
    Everyone telling me Consortium's new star general
        curious about her name, *Sherronda.*
            I want to meet her. I don't dare call Bramah.
            Soon, I'll burn these notes.
            Soon, the drones will see only
                acceptable words: *Un coup de dés!*

## MESSAGES & ENCAMPMENT

*Hidden in the Redwood Forest*

Wrong in every epoch, evacuees
when Consortium fell, splinter groups ran
toward any season's Portal Opening;
many rued the day the Dry extended,
wildfires and toxic smoke, chemicals—
Settlers cleared vine maples and Douglas firs.
We'd heard Pacifica, a better place.
We whispered stories from the Before-Time.
Last stands of timber, Perimeter grown.
To get through the gates, we sold our children.
Odds on favourites, skilled craftswomen, escaped.
*We'll not be wanted even when we build.*
No one open to hearing their auguries.
*Ghosts roam stolen land, time brings affliction.*
Our sayings disregarded, dismissed, then——
Came the times, and the times were bad,
Bramah's arrival unnoticed by most.
Our hands outstretched, we gave her parchment scraps:

*The Baker of Kingsway Waylays Messages*

He was known far and wide, praise singer
rough hands covered in flour, sometimes sawdust
mixed in with the flour, flour sometimes mixed
with boll weevils baked into bread—we ate mouthfuls
happy to hear his songs, sung in Gujarati, in Cantonese,
as translated by the Itinerant Scribe
T-LOHK, the Last of Her Kind.
From time to time, we'd see her on the heels
of Bramah, as she searched with Raphael.

Here is what T-LOHK wrote then posted
on Cy-Board #6:

This city rubble,
lonely as broken glass,
paper bits, dust 'n diesel,
plastic smouldering to bubble,
pockets drop, knees skinned,
this evening fragrant—
Seed Savers whisper rumours; from the east
comes a warrior, Sherronda, on hire.
Will she bite the hand that feeds?

This story thrice repeated, Sherronda
infamous general intent on order
transport traders bartered tales of her
brown rice for guns, guns for fuel
this tale, Ahmedabad to Baghdad
Baghdad to Shanghai
flown over and across, transport planes
migrants rendered
back to Kingsway, snuck in across Perimeter.
Just north of here, each checkpoint unlocked by,
well, we are never supposed to name her——
Abandoned in the street that time forgot
lurid Akebono gnarled trunks lichen
scales shrivelled under mossy clumps, fungi
yielding spores not to be inhaled or else!
Ramshackle houses sinking, cracked concrete.
Under petals falling came a stranger
father to the son, they called him Bartholomew.

# TROUBADOURS SING OF BARTHOLOMEW & HIS TIMES

Seasons decaying, supply chains fading.
He worked with Seed Savers to farm harvests.
He learned the trades, iron ploughshares, the wheel.
He devised symbols for travellers on the road
migrants, refugees, outcasts—
safe passage through the use of carved symbols.
Doorway lintels, tavern benches, shadows
a bumblebee, a hexagon, chevrons.
*Oh be not anxious*
*although our meetings, banned.*

We will find them inside the battle-worn
bombed-out bridges, forgotten railway shacks,
picked up and later challenged to enter
six gates, a city's perimeter, the crowd will cry,
*Insistence.* A reserve army. Our labour.
*Who could have imagined*——
Consortium embattled, street chaos
warriors from the east hired to control
Pacifica to Mexico, killings
transport planes running on the dregs of fuel
supply chains fragile as daisy chains—broke—
    demolished factories where once
    thousands worked pottery, earthenware
from gate to gate, women sold their bodies
    desperate for food, margins to the centre,
the city, traversed by train, pinnately compound
Ahmedabad, honey locust leaves burned.
Bartholomew said to be imprisoned
black-hooded, slated for the axe, then saved.
Consortium needed literate heroes.

Outside Perimeter's gates, crowds gathered:
a collect of weary Resisters roamed,
non-GMO seeds sown into their rags
pine cones, scattered, burnt offerings, spells cast.
Paris, the river Seine, many more killed.
After the fires, the death of the honeybee.
*Un coup de dés, jamais jamais.*

## BRAMAH DECIPHERS SEED SAVER SCRAPS

Orphaned at birth, tucked in a coracle
sent down a river in Old Pacifica
found by Guards of the Fifth Gate and trained
commanders quick to promote his learning
under fire he just put his head down
conflicting orders, he never complained.

Not many remembered the young scholar
survivor of Migrant Camp #3.
Lover of—father to—names left unsaid.
*Only the locksmith knows for sure,* we said.
Oak box findings, pieces of a chalice.
Perchance, a ring, gold engravings
      the letter *B*.

# PARTIAL TRANSCRIPT #1: KINGSWAY CORRIDOR

*Raphael Interviews Illegal Migrants, Outskirts of Perimeter*

Yes, it's true, we came to believe in ugliness:
our lips, nose, gait, clothes,
the clothes most of all.
            If outside Perimeter, we didn't get supply,
                no quick fix, online luxe for us!


Far distant any arms of charity, reclaimed.
Fear, our friend, we were told to proclaim,
*The New Normal Will Work Out.*
We just laughed and coughed and boarded our bus,
            we jam-packed them trains, sometimes masked.

From the position of bastard,
illegitimate. *As we came into this world—*
Well, isn't that what their Good Book said?

What's that? No, we never saw him, this name
*Bartholomew* means nothing to us.

Anyway, as we were saying,
already make-believe, not sanctioned,
unrecognized, unofficial.

Outside—
Perimeter.

# PARTIAL TRANSCRIPT #2: ONCE WERE TOWER JUNIPER

*Raphael Interviews a Handful of Survivors*

Deep inside Perimeter.
Houses on large lots,
abandoned when the bombs struck.

Cedar, hemlock, mountains mist-drenched.
Pacifica, the S-zone,
where rain would fall, unburning.

Told to save parts, we did, for them——
What was that? You mean the man they call Bartholomew?
No, we only seen him once.

He told us to resist. We didn't know—
well, you see how it is now, what we've done——

their privately owned generators,
machines inbuilt

just in case. And now it's come to this,
this survival, is a mode of operation,
operating, this mode is living
just—Bartholomew, you say?
Maybe he got taken. You know, rendered.
Them transport planes, grain embargoes lifted.
Maybe he got lucky, Pacifica to Paris,
         if you can call it that——

♕

Two days later, when interrogated,
a Guard of the Fifth, weary and on the take,
mumbled head down to an outraged Tribunal
 something about, *Yes, a locksmith*
  *well, I thought she was on hire, right?*
*Them transport planes, low fuel, how to keep track*
 *okay, maybe there were also a conscript*
  *couldn't tell, his face covered in dust.*

# WORD REACHES BARTHOLOMEW

*Sighted,* said that baker once Kingsway at Wessex
sifting flours, his hands powdery white
transported, chain-ganged to Paris
*once were Rue Mouffetard,* cobblestone streets
with each turn of his dough, he quoted verse:
*City of Interiors, ghost workers*
*Before-Time enfilade, a series*
*Seen him more than once,* said that baker, smiling.
        *Here, fold this*—crisp strudel or puff pastry
*I do all Kul/Chewers,* he'd say, lisping.

Fishmongers called out in Cantonese
        some kid from Hubei shipped in, his mask torn
passersby nodded, beggar boys darted, to snatch and steal.
*Seen him,* said the tinkers, *well before dawn,*

all the other street vendors laughing too—
        One day an old Irish tinker said,
*That boy? He carried an old oak box.*
*That box, been with him forever,*
*maybe even one day, he will unlock—*

Then the Tinker and the Baker laughed,
*That boy? He'd stand streetside, never missed a thing.*

*Strong lad, that boy, always talking trade, concrete dust.*
After his night shift at Consortium,
arms and hair covered in slag-ash-dust,
he'd look into the half-open door, bakeshop ovens blazing.

Said Bartholomew to the Tinker and the Baker,
*If you hear of him again——*
Outside, beggar boys sang, sweeping wet streets,
*Vega, Draco, we never going back.*

# BARTHOLOMEW'S SECRET, RECOUNTED IN SONG

Always the Guards ask me, *Which one is she?*
Abigail, shape-shifter, strawberry blonde
long or short, young or old, travelling my heart.

Her Aunties and her farm, epoch to age:
*Always reckon on an A in our home.*

Always the Guards ask me, *Which one is she?*
Abigail, shape-shifter, strawberry blonde
long or short, young, or old, travelling my heart.

We'd laugh then and her lips tasted of wine——
*Abigail, Abigail, travel my heart:*

You bore me a boy; you tore us apart.
Abigail, shape-shifter, strawberry blonde
your hair in my hands, your song in my heart.

The next day Bartholomew met his long-lost son.

## REUNION IN PARIS

No one left alive to see us survive.
Our form strange, invisible but present.
    *Absence our presence is,*
    *strangeness our grace—*
Silk-threaded words, woven, twisted, then turned.
Théâtre de la Huchette, where we met.
Winter, spring, summer, fall as once were called.
We relayed to Bramah when she found us.
Grandmother's sayings both pithy and wise:
*Choose action over thought, as best you can.*
*Leaven action with just enough intent.*
Bramah smiled, said nothing, bent to her tools.
We gave her a document. She thanked us,
street criers proclaimed, *Bartholomew's Rule.*
We warned Bramah of the warrior woman.
Triumphant, she'd march east to west, filming
all her exploits transmitted, Big E posts.

Everywhere we turned, a film crew, busy.
Two ex-Guards of the Fifth, now on hire.
Everywhere the name *Raphael*, windblown.
Everyone wanting to be present when
    at long last, father and son reunited.
Someone said *On the banks of the river Seine.*
Others claimed in a courtyard with plane trees,
    shadowed by the groaning hulk of a bombed-out
        cathedral, lavender loaves burning on cobblestone.
Past midnight in a tavern the film crew
    tossed drinks, and said, *Yes,*
        *tears in his eyes.*
        *Un coup de dés!*

# BRAMAH ARRANGES AN ESCAPE

*Overheard in Café Mallarmé*

Guard: Where are the numbers, incident comprised of—

Préfecture: That safe house identified.

Informant: We saw no one escape, we saw no one.

Préfecture: Evening is occurrence. That Itinerant Scribe
T-LOHK. Arrested.

*Again. Crowds gather;*
*the river in October, as once was called,*
*close to mid-month, a trajectory—*

Informant: I tell you I never knew their names.

—one woman, short of stature, perhaps mute?

—trades satchel hung loose from her shoulder.

—one man, greying red hair, a foreign national for
sure;

—and with them a strapping lad, huge shoulders, covered
in dust.

Heard outside the Paris Perimeter,
a roaming gang of beggar children sing:
*Un coup de dés, un coup de dés, jamais.*

## THE LONG MARCH FROM THE NEW NORMAL

Gods to bubble up
        mud-placated
we would be forced
        those long journeys
forever and a day
        the days
forced themselves
        journeymen
foot soldiers, every empire
        mud-spattered
marching forever
        women enlisted
when the men ran out
        long hours
gods abandoned, revived
        days when thirst
the distance between two lips
        transport planes
no seats just ozone
        jumpers
no one to placate fear
        the days so long
land to ocean and over
        journeywomen
soldiers and called her
        Iraq, Baghdad, Green Zone
Queen of the Nile, Euphrates
        that cradle, Consortium forced us, and we became survivors of
            the long—mud everywhere, marching—

# BATTLE TO BEGIN THE RULE OF THE GOOD

>>>>>>

♕ ♕ ♕

If only a fortnight longer, Bramah——
We are close to victory, a new day dawns.
Locksmith and scholar stood arm's length apart.
Open at their feet, an old oak box, waiting——
Bramah's long black braid sweeping the smooth wood.
Bartholomew, you must end this war now.
His once-red hair streaked grey, eyes burning bright:
Soon we'll end it, and we'll end hunger, too.
You'll help us won't you, you'll use your powers?
Bramah sighed and shook her head, heart heavy.
Don't you see, Bartholomew, this will end—
In ruin? he said, with a rueful smile.
When Consortium fell, it fell for lack——
no food, no seasons, no turning time back.

Said Bramah to Bartholomew:
Avoid slogans, avoid cant.
They were the two of them standing tent-side
Pacifica to Paris—back again.
Sunlight glinting on armour, bare-headed
Bartholomew the Good, they once called him.
Resisters loyal no matter what happened.
Parapet to battlefield they followed.
Bramah said, Avoid marching in parades.
Learn to make things, to grow things, save seeds.
Her words drowned out by the clamour of war.

And so then to raise armies, they parted,
Bartholomew and Raphael eastward.
First, Ahmedabad, mission to conquer
oil, ancient gates, munitions, secret spells.
Bramah in sadness told Bartholomew,
*Keep him safe, your son, and trust that I will*——
Fate, chance, free will, the luck of the draw, swirled
dry and papery as oak leaves falling—
choice, to win freedom, to die by the sword.
Bartholomew and Bramah, that oak box,
both of them bent to stroke its smooth corners.

And did she leave them then, father and son?
And did she pledge to find the Lost Seasons?
Our eavesdropping, no match for her silence,
she with her lock and her key, turning——
*Such riches the Seasons each twig and leaf*
*on the threshold of, gone forever more*
*once was, and used to be, green turning grey*——

Sakura blossoms, fat pink bunches, fell
dogwood petals, creamy carved cups, brown-tinged
honey locust, tight green furls, about to——
——open——
Bartholomew to his fate—
Bramah through that other gate.
Portal of the Lost Seasons, mission's quest
under guise of a Consortium contract:
logistical supply chain IT codes
satellite to satellite, seeds and food
production monitored remote, pirated
warring factions of the Tribunal wresting
control away from the centre, margins
on the march, chaos in a time of want.

Bramah contemplated power and chance.
Her plan to hijack Consortium's goals.
Demigoddesses, though, can be fallible.
Furious winds of an angry planet jabbing—
throwing up rogue portals to different times.
On her mind a mission to fight evil.
In her heart, an ache for that brave beggar
boy last seen seated in Royal Baghdad.
*He fell to his doom and now saves us all!*
Fate or free will, a roll of dice, tumbling
Bramah headfirst into a portal trap
realizing almost too late her chance
to journey to the Court of Al-Rashid.
For there he sat, bent over a chessboard
boy with pieces fingered in hands gone numb
endless Eternal Game, each move, century
to epoch, holding off climate disaster
the boy and the caliph, staving off change:
ground ozone, knight to bishop, save the queen
East Antarctic Ice Shelf, protected pass.
Heard faint throughout the marble corridors:

> *Pieces of a chalice, parchment scraps boxed*
> *Un coup de dés, oak box to iron fence, jump!*

♛ ♛ ♛


We, always present, still unseen.
Travellers, migrants, foot soldiers, refugees
we, left behind; we, chained on buses.
Reserve army of labour finding
crumpled bits of paper, melted bullets.
We recalled and remembered Bramah's songs.

Somewhere, a bird singing, two downward notes
the last robin alive, perhaps, single poplar
silver leaves burnt brown falling, cottage eaves
sunk, caved roof, abandoned hearth, one table
built before, surface split, scarred, once oak, oiled
left behind, a single porcelain cup, gilt-
faded edge, cracked lip, empty of liquid
companion to a rose, transparent stem.
Outside, sakura blossoms, neon pink
tainted gene code—harmed—lift and swirl.

### Faint Echoes Heard

—once were called *Sakura*—April, May—
    first flowers, sparse stars, the spaces between
then deep rich pink bunches, fat poms falling—
    Magnolia, fur buds hooked, soon to rot
smooth petals—magenta to brown, fading—
    June heavy headed scent, peony-rose
spicy, vibrant after rain, full sun loved.
    Secret honey locust, oak leaves, lime-green
emerald to fainter hues, pinnate and slow.
    Unfurl to me your sweet fading ways, come!

Wars and accelerated, famine-flood
Bramah worked to turn, file, click, tap and thumb.
Scroll, press—soft undertones, as if words might
call forth bud to blossom again——

*The honeysuckle and the rose*, sang Beggars and Swords,
    who trailed always behind Bramah, and we, also:
        *Once were, once was, jamais, jamais*—

# PART TWO

>>>>>>

>>>>>>

>>>>>>

# The Fall of Consortium in the Year 2105

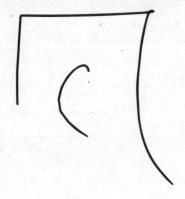

## BRAMAH AND THE YEARS BETWEEN

Far-future portal traveller, back and forth.
Witness to the end of the Four Seasons,
she never gave up searching for the boy.
Once, she'd looked high and low for Raphael
then found his father Bartholomew; charged
both to help the Seed Savers' Uprising,
uncertain about outcomes, pushing on
intent on the search for the Beggar Boy's
gap-toothed grin, shoelaces untied. She'd set
such a young person on an impossible task
to help save the world, not foreseeing rogue
portals, jealous to snatch and whisk and whirl
the Beggar Boy now seated at chess ♛
*Have you seen a young boy playing the game?*
she'd ask each year—messages arriving
tucked in tree trunks. Beside still waters one
midnight she crouched, brown hands smooth pliable
black hair, one braid long. Beeswax candle, lit
by a golden match, her smile illuminating
cursive scripts. Grandmother's secrets sent far
from the Valley, migrants on transport planes.
*Before it's too late, Bramah, come here quick.*
*Bring your codes for oak and for glass, hurry!*
Water reflections trembling silver light——

When we last heard word of her, on contract
Consortium locksmith for hire, codes
broken with a flick of her wrist, oak box
retrieved, stolen again, Big E, seeds, gold.
She took their mission, brought in their receipts
always found ways, never found out, her smile
fleeting, quick as her hands: *I'm for the good,*

her laughter echoing alleys to planes,
sly and kind, quiet and brave, no traces found.
Except we knew where to wait, Six Oaks' Wood.
Said the Aunties at the old well, crooning
*Names sprung from her fingers, sapling settlers—*
*Earth and her eons will encrypt her gait.*
>>>>>>
♛ ♛ ♛

*Let all evil die and the good endure.*

# PACIFICA IN THE DRY, SPRING PORTAL ABANDONED

First, drought because of accelerated.
Ghost traces, palimpsests, fragments crumbling
emanations, faint echoes, towers fell.
Fleeting glimpses, half-remembered, lost roads.
No one brave enough to say, *Climate Change!*
Then, that's all anyone spoke, stunned at loss
shivering when once were warm, or wilting
when once were temperate, fierce windstorms blew—
sideways, slant, close to invisible lines
faulted, cracked, sinkhole deep, tree roots exposed.
We learned to pause—bending toward moments:
fleeing Guards into corner stalls, hands against
walls, fingers lifting scraps of paper, dust
forbidden archives, dimly lit libraries
all the records, files, data, codes, locked tight.
Bombed basements, broken shards, long-forgotten
boxes stacked, put away, folders mislabelled
letters, diaries, witness to these events.
Then famine because of drought, food wars grew.
House to house, unrest slouching Dry to Wet
structural erosion, famine to the wars,
Perimeter unable to provide
capital any longer, nor any shops.
Come the day when Bartholomew would rise.
Reluctant warrior Sherronda his guide.

>>>>>>
♛ ♛ ♛

*Douglas fir, Six Sisters, furrowed bark deep.*
*Pine cones split to the seed, conifers' gift.*
*Branches, tresses, downward longing and sweep!*

We heard these lines in our sleep, then forgot.
We stuffed our pockets with document husks.

# CONSORTIUM LOSES CONTROL OVER THE SEASONS

In the Dry, grass bleached white, leaves shrivelled crisp.
Tree branches fell, sharp agro stench wafted
weak breezes in from the Valley, acrid
fumes, when petrol gangs salvaged fuel.
Dust everywhere, sunrays knifing our sight,
triggering alarms, *five-star-heat-dome doomed*,
chanted children, mouths parched, nails bitten quick.
Deep inside Perimeter, mansions blew
iced air, fed by drones humming, Big E on.
Everyone wary of overnight highs——
scissors in hand, our beggar children snipped
a thousand pages in exchange for food.

As ordered by Consortium brokers:
documents reassembled, then hidden.
Months to be determined, but how we asked,
keepers of time, cycles disrupted, trees:
rare finds, searched for and revered, inscriptions
carved, rubbed, memorized, mapped as wayfinders.
*Spring will not wait the loiterer's time*, sighed
bark and burl, furrows to the seed, dried husks
*who keeps so long away*——
Child labourers cut as they sighed and sang
bloodied fingers caressing ICC
reports, charts, data stacks, preserved numbers,
*from you have I been absent*—hands to eyes
asking as they shredded, *What is April?*

*Portals and Vortex*, we answered.
Consortium ordered us to ban mention of the weather.
We cited statistics from the Before.

Forcefield events, each of us carried scars:
thrown, spun, sucked, tossed, downward spirals, dark depths
waters, the weight of tears, unshed and stored
for the passing of temperate, for the ending of green.
Our hands reaching upwards, fingertips grazing
wavelengths of spent air—deaths marked in time
numbers, names, threaded into dates, then lost.

## PERILOUS EQUATIONS INSIDE PERIMETER

Everything happened much faster than planned.
The Dry, more severe and extreme, lasted.
Decade by decade windblown soil, crops failed.

Monthly Meat Feasts provoked long lineups.
Supermarket parking lots, staged raffles.
Our mouths salivated, remembering——

Injected Butterball Turkeys, rare steaks.
Scrounging abandoned stores, we hoarded tins.
These were the good old days compared to the Dry

when Water Cartels took over cities.
Settlers drained too many lakes, drilled too deep.
Concrete, tarmac and steel over marshes.

Soon we were waiting days for one hour
when the leaking pipes turned on
pressure matched to income; our levels, low.

>>>>>>
♕ ♕ ♕

# THE END OF MONEY

It were all about meat, plants, herbs and cheese.
Enough sticks and chopped wood: Big E rations
grass to graze, and grains to feed, cattle, goats
always looking out for mutated parts——
rustic revival relearning old skills
when *good with our hands* meant enough to eat.
We became hoarders of everything thrown
bartering for scraps—wool, cotton and tin
plywood and plastic, shards of glass, steel gears
cutlery knives, scissors and safety pins.
One day we raided a department store
riches on every floor and then we met
old men and women who'd lived on the sixth
once were the realm of appliances sold.

Migrants from the Hidden Valley, guild trails
secret passageways, underground tunnels
old viaducts, abandoned culverts, roads
cut rough rip-rap from hills, mountains laid waste
industrial power plants long unused
            these were the People of the Sixth
some would stay true to the Uprising's aims
some would later join online mobs, *convoys*
Seed Savers bemoaned, *easy Wi-Fi codes*,
handed out by Tribunal executives
eager to hire mercenaries, Guards
deserted their posts for Big E tickets
a year's worth of energy, satellites
beaming access to Before-Time luxuries.
We, the ones left behind, infiltrated
by miscreants known as R & G Inc.
*Follow the money*, they said with a wink.

We stared at them, then looked around our store
once was founded, a company, fur, skins
trading post as conqueror, now refuge.
Shelves empty, walls pockmarked with gunfire.
We found tucked in crevices these fragments:

**Seed Savers' Rendezvous**

Before-Time forest, settler imported:
Douglas fir, oak, poplars, sumac and ash.
Vine maples, settlers' clearing, bivouacked.
Last stand timbers in Perimeter.

**Songs of the Seed Savers' Rebellion**

*—the honeysuckle and the rose,* we sang,
drifters caught, unmasked. Free trade zones shut down.
For the good of all, we believed, skeptics
yet driven by hunger to succeed.
*—go to the seeds when they are ready,* pick
dry, save, find the space, store them well
*—pluck, rub, shake, grab, cycle to season,* watch!
Barter and hoard, trade and share, we'll survive.
Cycle to season, rub; safe seeds to arrive.

*When we, the people, get hungry enough,*
feet marching in unison, unshod chants,
Sherronda's Army of the Just, eastward
ever eastward to the Gates of Baghdad.

And when we, the people, angry, afraid—
some will rise in ignorant rage storming
a few will speak quiet, searching for good
*no farmers, no food,* we'll all want to say

hired hands, refugees, migrants and convicts
flotsam and jetsam, underclass pining
for better days, for new normal returns.

### Consortium Collapse as Recounted

Last of the Executive Council fled,
HQ Concrete, pentagon-shaped, where once
dyes, pharmaceuticals, magnesium,
warehoused semiconductors, abandoned.
Six square wings, paternoster elevators
Perfect for the two Guards left behind.

Cleanup crew multi-skilled, bright-eyed and shrewd.
Mercenaries on hire, quite clever:
Rajancrantz & Gabbarbhai, Gujarati
sons whose mothers wed colonels.
Rajancrantz part Norwegian, Gabbarbhai
DNA cocktail, prized test-tube baby:
cadets to Guards of the Fifth, free agent
status granted early, eager to serve
pretty much any boss who paid them well.

Deep in the HQ library, found:
a film studio, intact, reel to reel
eight-track to digital, cameras restored.
Up and down the paternoster lift, chained
compartments inch by inch, looped up and down,
Rajancrantz would dictate to Gabbarbhai
film ideas about the things they saw.

Consortium broken, food wars amok,
supply chains shattered, natural gas lines lost,
wealthy nations hoarded vaccines, food, oil.

Agro chemical factories attacked by Seed Savers.
A new Dark Ages that Consortium could not control.
Our warrior Sherronda will sort things out.
We'll cast the hero of the Resistance:

Bartholomew. ⬡

And then out in the streets, the things they heard:

    They told us to use less, them from their homes
    Perimeter Enclave, electric cars
    all their machines certified green and good
    us in our Rentalsman, we did what we could.
    They partied on, bed-hopping, pill-popping—
    *Perimeter Mansions,* we called that zone
    wide, spacious boulevards, timed sprinklers gone.
    *Iron and stone,* we whispered.

### Stories from the Threshold

Under shade of a young pine tree, we crept—
forbidden to water—and yet we hauled
pre-dawn, under cover—smoky sky drift.
Before-Time plastic buckets, cracked, rag-patched.
We'd trekked for miles outside Perimeter
forged transit papers, lost, long expired.
To stand before slender tree trunks, split bark
tiny plums, misshapen, blue veins showing
sparse growth, thin skin, leaves curled green, grey.
Shade hunters, breeze followers, water divined
water stolen from Consortium tanks.
Water payments hoarded, body barters
endured for the sake of capfuls, droplets
saved from the last air-conditioned offices——

Perimeter families sat down to lunch.
Their sprinkler-fed lawns, lush, welcoming play.
Widescreen TVs, indoor patio Guards
hired from the Fifth Gate, time cards, twice stamped.
After dessert, toddlers blew soap bubbles.
Supply chains shrunken, though robust enough
to plan the best getaway vacations.
Booster shots for their arms, six months apart.
Anyway, they employed many of us.

### Seed Savers' Method as Repeated for a Generation

Endings so sudden and catastrophic
we didn't have time to select our seeds
grabbed, shoved into canvas: pods and kernels
storage obsessed: Mason jars always best.

Heard faint, through a dark cobbled alley, clattering
two beggar boys running,
*Now we are here*
*and so we will remain,*
*should have jumped that fence*
*should have wished for rain.*

## ONCE WAS SUMMER

Outside Rentalsman, the sun beat down hard.
Air-conditioned rooms sold off long ago.
Draperies, Venetian blinds, roll-up shades:
stolen, traded, degraded; fans sold out.
Glass towers without electricity.
We searched for cool rooms, broke into basements.
Hot air as the day rose north by due east.
Broken windows, roof overhangs fallen
dead trees, crumbled awnings, missing shutters.
Once, gambrel and hood, once trellis and vines.
Once, aluminum and slatted, rolled down
once spacious porches, wraparounds with mint tea.
A generation who could remember
benign light——children laughing, joyful sounds.

No greenness, local tree canopy gone.
Buildings jam-packed, adjacent concrete towers.
Private libraries closed, roadblocks, armed Guards.
Year over year, underfunding of shade.
We organized our own fire brigades.
Older children sent; ambulance crews helped.
*What side of the buildings are they on?*
*What floor and were they alone and using?*
These were the questions we taught them to ask.
Aunties walked miles before sunrise with masks.
*Wishing Well water clean and free,* they'd laugh.
No tongue tasted sweeter, or limbs refreshed.
Beggars and Swords marched, ripped pages to wet
foreheads, who tended to the sick, no regrets.

At the end of the Spring Portal, no rain
smoke-wreathed sun or a killing matchless blue.
Perimeter gardens withering, sparse
ration cards meaningless, food depots scarce.
Grandmother in her high meadow hideout
fingers on her beads, beeswax candles lit.
She sent wordless message to Bramah.
She hung garlands of roasted milk thistle.
She swept and swirled dry dust into glass jars.
Fieldworker, she crumbled herbs into earth.
Barefoot, bareheaded, she buried keys, locks
two-fold petition to the Sky Gods, clear
intent, to plead for rain, to call Bramah home again.
Arms outstretched, over soil barren of grain.

*Found Pinned on a Cy-Board, Hologram:*
tattered, fading, a scrap of paper

>>>>>>>>>>>>>>>>>>>>>>>>>>

our Ambulance Hall, saved from the Before-Time
*We have left with ourselves,*
and our pets, with family.

Everyone scrounging for anything round
scraps of cloth, old hats, cracked buckets to dip
shallow ponds, the lee side of old wells, pumps
abandoned cisterns, parched, parted lips—

We couldn't even say the word *water.*

Cats in feral colonies, nighttime friends
who slunk and hunted rats, then disappeared.
Then the Great Hunger came.

# FIRST THE FARMERS, THEN THE SOIL

Farmers, day labourers, truckers,
care aide workers, a few nurses.
No doctors left outside Perimeter
save those in chains. Against all odds,
without access to, and starving
in the Wet and in the Dry,
banned gatherings held, everyone masked,
they pleaded for supplies; rogue bandits haggled hard,
scarce resources, everyone willing, eager for their jab,
trouble was, no medicines to be had——
*Driven to soap and sunlight, our burns sting.*
*One day we'll be famous for glass-making.*
They created caucuses, committees,
sit-ins, marches; parading they filled streets
agitating for land, they wanted what they tilled,
harvest redistributed, fair portions,
wages from the earth, reaped that they should keep.
*Grasses once thigh-high by now*, farmers said.
        *Once*, they said, when oaks grew green,
        roots warmed by a nurturing sun,
        rain-fed, winter-spring-summer-fall—
        each followed the next, we were in balance,
        plantings, harvest, we could take and be safe.
        *Our dominion over*, they said.

No sooner than these words uttered,
winds rose and blew even more soil away,
withered white grasses, parched ground underfoot.
*Jumped the Fence*, moaned the farmers.

# THE GREAT HUNGER

>>>>>>
♛ ♛ ♛

—because of
accelerated climate change, drought—
    because of drought, then the floods,
    then the fire, because of the fire
    famine, and because of famine,
        food wars, riots, the soil blasted
        blown, because the soil gone
        farmers killed themselves—
    because the earth, lost, and the farmers dead,
        their daughters, Seed Savers.
    Because the Seed Savers, resistance.
    Because Resistance, uprising, *jaldi, jaldi*
    Because the people, although famished,
    Because the people, bellies distended, bones bleached,
    seeds still saved, because the seeds saved, Uprising,
    because we rose, because we, *jaldi, jaldi*
the fall of Consortium. Like that—

## The End of the Pacific Rainforest

Northward expansion, high-pressure ridges.
Each year longer, persistent heat domes pushed
away rainstorms, deflecting marine air.
*Once were temperate,* they'd say in villages.
Once were mighty cedars, Douglas fir stands
clinging to solitary days of rain.
Each year they sent scientists to measure
high temperatures, forests all aflame.
Large tracts of land rendered inhabitable.
Black pine beetle, ferocious windstorms, drought.
And with the drought, the food dried up, parched soil.
Dry memories, failed crops, misshaped buds fell.
Water an obsession, bartered, traded.
*Two thousand five hundred,* those miles all gone
survivors chanted, *the weight of the wrong.*

At night, Beggars and Swords mounded soil to the roots
        first the drought then the food
            supply chains broken.
    *Come Bramah, come Bartholomew*
        *banish evil, bring us the good.*

# BEFORE-TIME HUNGER SCRAPS

## *As Saved by the Itinerant Scribe T-LOHK*

875–884 1097–1162–1230–1231–1275–1299
1315–1317–1333–1337–1396–1407
1601–1603 1618–1648 1630 1640–1643 1648–1649
1651–1653 1661 1690 1693–1694 1696–1697
1709 1738–1756 1740–1741 1769 1943
1788 1798–1793 1804–1872 1913
1810 1811 1846 1849 1811–1812 1816–1817 1846 1867 1873 1879
1845–1849 1866–1868 1870–1872 1876–1879
1878–1880 1888–1892 1891–1892 1895–1898 1896–1902
1914–1919
1919–1922 1928–1930 1932
1924–1925 1940–1945
1946–1947
1959–1961 1967 1968 1972–1974
1975–1979 1984–1988 1992–1998–2000
2004 2003–2005 2005–2006 2012 2016–2017–2022

## *Eyewitness Testimony*

*They dug as directed, parched soil, upturned*
Once the rain poured down and we would gather
kneeling to pray, under wet cedar boughs.
Settlers, we stole the land; yet still felt awe.
We overheard the locksmith, Bramah, say;
*The last wheelwright*
*All the things I was a part of—now gone*
no tremor in her hands, voice clear, quiet
working the wood, axe, saw, mallet, chisel.
Ciswen the Blacksmith to make metal tips;
two women working at lathe and at the forge.

### The Dry Lament

Everything we love will be taken soon
plane tree in Rentalsman, shade-giving friend
withered dried leaves, cracked bark, spare branches snapped.

### Scarcity a Demarcation

Garden fountains turned on after curfew
Consortium families under floodlights
children kicked soccer balls on painted grass.

### Beggars and Swords Remembered Old Songs

Month's end, hidden portals, leading to sound.
Oh find us again: Four Seasons, temperate —
where once we took wild plants to help and heal.
Dandelion nettles, elderberries steeped.
Rosehips eaten raw, twigs and roots, gone.

## POSTED TO CY-BOARD #6

*Tattered Foolscap, yellow lines bleeding old ink:*

The story disappeared. Bramah chanted it back into existence.
Then she ate the words. Then they fell out. She kept on going.

At month's end, the moons, two pale crescents, she met them again.
The words, branched, reeds tufted by the river's edge.

The words, soothsayers, embedded seeds, sprouted news.
Bramah bent her head and listened.

Up the banks on either side, two armed camps.
Pennants fluttered in a southeast wind.

When Bramah straightened to meet the eyes of men,
not one Seed Saver nor scientist met her gaze.

*Trouble on the wind,* sighed the locksmith. True enough.
*I've seen it before. I know how to look.* And she did.

She fell in behind long lines of migrants—slow, sure steps—
by the time the moons were full, she knew what to find.

Nimble fingers to pick out, as if from the air, word-seeds.
Saved, tucked inside her pockets, *Raphael.*
First, though, stone by stone the path to show her—
Bramah, smiled, turned her head, *Bartholomew.*

## Bartholomew & Raphael Join the Uprising

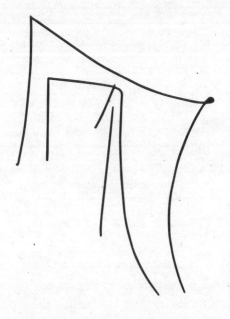

# T-LOHK THE SCRIBE ARRIVES WITH A WARNING

### *Bramah Sent Me with a Message*

Outside to be inside, Ahmedabad at night
unusual and unexpected strange rain
waters released. Ground, soggy underfoot
a gathering to read, although banned.
Enough light from a single lamp, street watchers
curfew not yet called. They spoke about water.
In the courtyard of the Last Rajah came a scribe
some knew as T-LOHK, mysterious stranger.
She sang to Bartholomew and Raphael
warnings from the Before-Time, the price of war.
*Hear me out, you who would rule for the good.*

>>>>>>
♛ ♛ ♛

### *T-LOHK's Ballad of the Before-Time Battles*

### *Battle Number One*

A September song as once was called.
We went to the cathedral to hear news.
See here before us these terrible times:
tribes, sects, cults, groups, family to family, wars
Consortium derivatives, stocks paid.
That campaign in the east, arms trading,
      oil dredged, fracked, transported, containers full.
In the year of the reign 2100—
And listen, and write down this,
      a church sanctuary, after all.
        We recounted the past, all the places

and saw vivid Beirut, where once mother—
        those dresses flown in, Ahmedabad
and saw us foreign correspondents.
Listen to our words: Northern Ireland, Portugal, Iran
Afghanistan, the First Gulf War, Algeria and civil.
And hear us echo, that chant, *Sabra/Shatilla.*

*No meanings suggested for these moments,* we said.
And heard Sunni, where once our family, believers.

## Battle Number Two

All our declarations, predetermined
boundaries, checkpoints.
Perimeter.
And given and taken.
A series of dictators
for demos.

We were speaking then of worlds created.
*Imagine—the road, Beirut to Damascus.*
This heard, decade to decade, era to epoch.
From sources crumbling in old libraries:

we found nurseries, rhyming games
Skye(s) and Picot, see these villagers rot.
To London Town, all the Ottomans.
O bring us French and the British,
bring us Lord Balfour.

Hooked to the last of the Big E, those plates
        hologram pictures flickering:
bulldozer, a-pushing, what once was border.

We were speaking then. Syria, Iraq.
Boundaries demolished.

After, emerging——headsets, flung, thrown off.
We shook our heads side to side sharp sunlight
              burning——

*Battle Number Three*

We were chanting ISIS
at the gate named Abelard
We were chanting *Hezbollah*
at the gate named Heloise——

As the sun set on our ever-presence
We wrote in Arabic the words for Sunni, Shia
We learned Turkish, Kurdish
We observed those drones flying Iran
We distinguished training missions,
destruction.

We spoke of evil and wicked.
We spoke of enslavement, those women.
We described a beheading
—eighty-four and Palmira. An archeologist.
We pointed, seven different camera angles
We shared that burning, encaged
a fighter pilot, Jordanian.

*They put his spectacles back on the severed head.*

We used the word *cult.*
We sang of a young warrior in Shillong
followers in the thousands, tapped stolen

Wi-Fi posts, searched for the real,
Calcutt to Baghdad, she amassed brigades.
Her *Bismillah!* Pop—
that old song—some called her Shanti-Ben, Sister of Peace.
Others named her Sherronda—
Her flashing eyes! Her snake-coiled hair!

*Battle Number Four*

We were then inside Damascus.
Smoke poured into the cathedral
Greek Orthodox, structural and standing.
We saw with our own eyes
the eyes of the saints, those dragons, too
        drilled obliteration
        a kind of terrible beauty.
We saw with our own eyes what the poet meant
        terribleness, being born
                transcendent—
We stood on the floor of the chapel.
We stood on a carpet of destroyed paintings
        such careful cuttings, strips of ancient canvas
                machine to shred, tape to measure
                precision, that thinness, exact.
Hundreds, hundreds! Our feet engulfed. Covered.
Our heads bare. We looked upward and saw
        nothing—well outside Perimeter, in the little towns.
Cotton spinning north of Cairo.

## Battle Number Five

—We spoke of the young warrior, now a general
who learned English by reading *Othello,*
        card gamer, at her side two mercenaries.

—We said, *No one any longer believes*
the land demarcated—
long line of refugees, on foot, fleeing. Time-old tradition, left-behind passports.
No intention of return.

—We sang of mass exodus, up from (E)urope.
And across—

—We warned everyone, Seed Savers to scientists, as a god-abandoned people
        among the believers.

## Battle Number Six

A rough beast slouches.
In the desert, a scratched surface—
        bones.

We saw them cross the Euphrates.
We saw their columns march to the church,
Old Armenian.
They had called in coordinates,
a bombing.
We hesitate to speak,
their digging—

That first slaughter, those bones
thrown into the streets.

# THE AHMEDABAD CANTOS

*As inscribed by T-LOHK the Scribe*
*culled from the lost library of Al-Rashid*
*small children, their fingers, pasting slender shreds*
*Baghdad to Paris, to this City of Gates.*
*Recited then, by the Makers of Ahmedabad*
*to Bartholomew & Raphael.*

♕

## All Sultanates, in the End

There we were, running for cover, chain-free
persistence; they called us *The Unlucky.*
There was something about her, we all said
Woman General followed by deserters.
*When will we be strong enough to look for—*
*Eckdom,* extreme, we searched weapons, *all their weapons.*
If anyone visits, *Kem Cho, Aao-Jo—*
In her cell, beaten: *Mun-nay, bo serus ché—*
Old woman, you don't know the half of it.
The metrics of her despair staggered us.
Looking back, we could see that— Night always:
we didn't even remember what we were—
worn, we scavenged: pinned, clipped,
gathered and torn.
Proclamations posted, interceptions.
In the Name of God, those generations.
We were of that, and recanted, and heard,
*What kind of law will govern us?* we asked.
We've heard of a great warrior in the east.
She would—Lost, long-ago photograph.

We never used to be like that and now:
To search for truth, to not find her, except
the linocut sheet pulled and stretched sun-wise.
Guards of the Fifth would watch us printmakers.
Feet: soles of, and the tongue, surface texture.
On the banks of the Sabarmati, we—
Light sheen of sweat. Eight stags running. Midnight.
Our hands, honey-covered, cupped, pulled. Our hair—
Outside Perimeter, Guards encircled.
Sweet almond oil, beeswax, hemp, stolen barter.
Charred, burnt, singed, the child. Somewhere, a robin—
Night. We stared: images from long ago.

## The Tale of the Rani of Jhansi

Close, that gate: *Bhadra*, the child said, rags hung
auguries the day we met, hail, lightning.
White pellets struck bronze cups, candy crystals.
Heads turned—he kept women inside his gaze—
that water, that mud, containers to spill
rubbed, lamplight circumference, that wooden block
keeper of hurts who sits by her well, hands—
Her hair lifts, breeze-catcher, knee bent, she trails
to heal, she told us, *to write out each tear.*
Packets of paper, sharp arrows sent down.
A thousand earbuds flung kissing the ground.
Outside the Well of Deep Forgetting, slaves.
This city, this river—*Aao-Jo*, they called
and told of the hare chasing a dog: hills
hidden, pinpoints, finger-locators, cut.
*Chakras*, those Guards who brought, twisted, her edge.
She had to create her own radiance.
Birds, stars, S-shaped locket tucked at her waist.
To pull on that golden string, wrist-wrapped round
*what hurts, what helps, what heals*
that sharp knife, chisel—to redraw relief.
And she was wrong about that, too, and wept.
Notched, chipped, a groove, on one side of the shank.
We kept telling her, she wouldn't listen:
*What good ever came of looking?* Those posts.
Other people, smiling life-aggregates.
Her eyes on his eyes, those girls: hair, hips, curve, lift.
Inscribed elbow to wrist, knee to ankle,
beat on, boats against such currents, ceaseless
kinetic chain, small print, blue grey injects.

You over there making new memories—she,
trapped prisoner of the revolution, red
and said each morning: *Dear ones, I am here*—

**From the Katubkhana of Pir Muhammad Shah**—

Those twelve gates, crescent, paisley, teardrops gold,
her instep rhythmic, his long lower back,
nights she would repeat: *Mozart, Vienna*—
the rest of her story is lost—some called her Scheherazade,
   unconfirmed, some say she roams as a wraith
      beseeching anyone to listen,
         absence, my presence is—

## At the Twelfth Gate, Ahmedabad After—

On the nature of gold, brass, that absence,
walking the parking lot of the Sandman.
In front, woman, arms raised, rain on asphalt.
She cried his name, said his name in her mind
that border space, sound not loud enough to
backward bend, cobra, corpse, that night two Guards—
She would recount a day's events, difference
His touch, skin to skin, year-long enclosure
Sadness, viscous, heavy spread through the town
Inside her, falling. Outside, snow, dropped. Children.
Don't you know how—can't you see, he'd never
*Muh-nay, boh deek che*—this she repeated.
Hair, eyebrows, lashes, lids, they were made to—
She would draw a line, city, transnationals
*Dear B*, those letters never sent—having
Alone in a basement apartment—found
old oak box, opened, a thousand words for slow
And asked, of images, what to lean to—
Dear diary, last year was so beautiful
Haunted: smiling, soft girls chanting until the rains
There they were, at the side of the river
Moon rising fat pink, riptide underneath
Washerwomen spoke of the Fisherman's Knot.
*This is journey*, they'd sing, *how we start home*
Shimmering silver liquid forever
all those killed, instant, shrapnel, everywhere
They would hold a great communion, thereby—
*O we have been away in the wars*, snow—
*Beauty, beauty*, cried their women in chains
That quiet quadrant, street ice, trees bare-branched.
*These years, and miles between us, your letters,*
*I could look at no one else for centuries.*

## The Charts of the World—

To find water we walked great distances.
Five-fingered push, pull, no give to our arms.
Outside, inside, Perimeter convoys.
Width, girth, length, our brown fingers around
morning: shots fired, blood pooling, white stone,
men crumpled, earth as acceptor of pain,
translucent memory. Before, a mirror, always
we saw, shadows drifting, ghost warriors.
At the tea shop called Ever After, we
traded stories of the Far East: Viet, the Congo,
Cambodia. Many arrivals, trans-
migrations, Belarus, Siberia—
We walked facing upward, hard-hearted moon,
those workers, that brittle barrier, predawn
five robins who chattered of Sherronda,
Warrior Queen, her sharp axe, her flashing eyes.
*Loneliness!* cried the roaming boy brigades.
All her curves, she'd soothe herself with S shapes.
We kissed her name, written there, our black books.
Forever after, our tired voices, asking.
*Geza-ah-Geza*, beggar children sang.
And so her name entered that morning twice—
Doomed warriors, those printmakers, we bent;
always, we were upstairs, pens to parchment—
Eight, then six, that wax extracted, saved scent.
As authorized, those lines, inlaid, cut, three
different stars visible, sea turtles, waves
in that street, we spoke of the seven hills,
terraced, classified, the way of stars, earth.
*Devanagari*, we whispered, fingers
to touch the plates, to prepare a surface
smuggled pages, cardboard, inked printing press,

different tonal effects, vibrant colours,
light passing to dark, grit mixed acrylic.
In this way we made thousands of scrolled maps.

## From Inside the Garden of the Murdered Katibs

Sweet cardamom tea, we sipped all night, lips—
Those underground chambers, where torture, where—
Tunnels, row upon row, photographs of—
Into a world not ours, we ventured, lost
and called those hours, *boudoir time*, where girls—
All softness, S-curves, hidden scars, applications.
Names written on the body without ink
and told again that story of—the way—
We would enter a room, every glance stored.
Louder, more elaborate, signs, gestures, codes.
And if drinking, even more still, our eyes
downcast, lash to line, leave-taking, their words.
Our names they said twice and asked us to stand.
Conqueror, invader, hard, long arms, legs and—
The rest of this story found only in
two vials, Pacific, Atlantic, we'd—

## Textile Workers, Karigars, Infiltrated, Radicalized

Carry cross borders, salted lips, tongue-tipped.
Months after that Battle, the Far Plains and—
*What pain is*, we sighed—our hands, tremor-filled.
Quartered, crescent and faint, those four trade winds.
*Thrown out like we were nothing*, we said, twice.
Languid, sinuous, we took our time swaying.
Others cried out, we knew this, our mouths shut.
Haunted faces, Before-Time lost-loves.
*Oh, to have found a way*, temperate, restored.

Resisted yearning, instead made things.
*About distances*, said the group—gathering
miles, rivers, oceans, mountains, those hills where—
About years, their kaleidoscope effect.
Inland, upcountry, on the coast, streetside,
lame children stood in a row, electron-
parts split upwards, snapped, discarded hundreds.
No one spoke the meaning of sacrifice.
*Darling, je reviens*, a woman whispered.
Slipped between those drifting worlds, silk birds, stars—
*Things we give up on*, sang the courtyard boys—
They sat cross-legged, nibs dipped, black ink, slant.
*Always look for the side-story*, said B.
That tattoo artist, damaged, he'd script,
*When those trade winds blow, who will protect us*—
Northeast to southeast, trinket to treasure.
Inside, a woman lifted her hips, curved.
Outside, that garrison, rifles from the East.
Those prisoners standing, knees to wall, heads bowed,
across the street, hidden library, we'd
found the room, bent to table, our fingers—
brush strokes low, and consistent on the plate.

## Pushed Up Against Khanjia Gate, the Last of the Resisters

Books written beginning to end, by hand—
This great gift given, this silence to see:
Only to learn Resistance fighters, gone.
After many months, those distances, vast—
The only thing from the past we wanted
       our loved ones
their faces, their voices, their hands, that time they said—
We are being disappeared, and drift between
      memory—a pink rose,
heathery lavender, plucked, pressed,
sometimes, a thousand years would pass or ten.
Foretold, far-seeing third eye, third moon's edge.
*You just think on that*, scolded the mother.
*Taro Nam Soo Che*, we asked again and—

      Time, cornered between two centuries, lit up—
*What kind of a people are you?* she asked.
Against fate she would create her own force:
      To save children from incarceration,
parents bartered with anything they owned.
Children crying, *so many of us gone*—
Always her fingers at the fork of wrong;
      somewhere wild, real, the other existed—
Obsessions: to overlay, to circle,
      that charnel house, desire, their small bodies.
Although a great many bombs fell, we worked
a bracelet of bright hair about the bone.
      Our backs bent toward paper, pencil, thumb—
Outside, horses jumped over dead ones, slashed,
      long-handled steel, flag of red cambric, tied
squeezed, beaten, reins blood-covered, chains, daggers.
      Inside Perimeter, inside that court:

We, printmakers, this scribe, her thick nub, thinned
all frailties that besieged all kinds of blood—

## The Beggars of the Four Ahmads Evoke the Tragic Tale of A & B

She held his gaze and said, *this.* They stood close.
Dipped pens, inks and prints, brushes, markers, these—
She longed to ask him about the eyes of—
A thousand horns to catch the call of arrows.
His jeans, that shirt, the fall of his hair, turned—
Sweat poured down between each horse, that slaughter.
Said the soldier: *I hit him on the chest*
*Everyone covered in blood, those long lines—*
With such force his skull caved in, the air was—
They no longer spread out and searched alone
Always, we are upstairs in the music—
These words and images, his voice recalled
What endurance meant, to live without, and
The way you changed me, feathers brushing skin
In that half hour just before dawn, when—
I looked at his site and found my name there
How could she be for joy amid despair—
Those broken concrete blocks, worms writhed in acid
Rain for days—inside the courtyard, a man
And calling, *Beauty, Beauty,* I lured him
To me, so I did make myself into—
From Arabia to Jerusalem—
And Damascus, southward from Syria
In the stillness of that desert, a man
Held together, torn apart, wind-scorched thirst
To dream, infinite, where groundwater
Always, upstairs, a man and a woman—
On her body, bitten, the marks of chains
Aftershocks for years, ghost tremors across

Towers, encampments where slum children worked
*Taro Nam Soo Che*, they asked each person
In that heat, unearthed, that frozen story—

♕

Bartholomew, hearing these words, wept.
Raphael said nothing, head bent, eyes downcast.

### The Tale of the Man Escaped from Turnaround Street, Culled Strands, Gathered from Lost Transcripts

Alaska: in the year of the reign [ ]. Spring.
No one was expecting that subduction—
*Inscribed on many: sing to us of change.*
Twisted, turned, the arms and legs of children,
at the corner of, they met to exchange messages.
Recalled those Guild Women, that swirl of paint
with each—they'd call out names, lost plants, lost species.
Each encounter, real, imagined, documented.
Consortium frantic to gauge damage.
Crumbling house at street's end, two lovers:
His hands on her breasts, his fingers inside—
Over the next five minutes, those ruptures—
See here, fault lines everywhere, dry to mud
landslides, desert prairies built up, flooded
Pacifica plains, Atlantic warming.
Once, men sang of five-hundred-year cod runs.
Look at me, from north to south, harbinger:
Shift-tilt of the Seasons, end of the Four.
Got my Time Traveller's Ticket the hard way.
Consortium sent me earthquake hunting.
Ground ozone measurements, they tried to quench
*Global ill-effects.* We called it earth's fury.

♛

Everyone shuddered at these words, T-LOHK
fingering shards of parchment, looked toward
Bartholomew, his eyes closed, his face, set
deep grooves between his brows, mouth downturned.
Raphael grimaced, shifted side to side
        and the Makers continued—

### On the Banks of the Sabarmati, in the Year—

We sang songs and cast-off children
chanted salt and street, *Hey chota, hey chota, jump!*
Whirlwind, fast rewind, forward. Tilt: those camps,
blasts, tattooed, *Harkat-ul-Jihad* on arms.
Inside the courtyard, that man that woman,
they trekked in from Jitali: *Nam Soo Che,*
wrote the woman known as Shanti-Ben
inquisitive about any strangers, she learned
they'd been transport prisoners from Pacifica,
released eastward as day labourers, indentured—
a series of Tribunal executives hired them as
cab drivers, rickshaw runners, nursemaids.
One of the woman pleaded write this down:
*in my mother's makeup cabinet only*
*one lipstick, coral vanilla and one*
*eyebrow pencil, a jar of face cream.*
These were Tales Told at Sundown as it were.
If in their dreams, a locksmith would appear
then they'd know to remember any questions.
The future: a black box sand-filled, shaken.
Said Shanti-Ben to the distraught migrants:
*Each wind blows across this earth sharp sweet salt.*
She amassed a following, loyal arms.
We declined. She shrugged her strong shoulders.
*Next time, then, in the coming troubles.*
*Everyone will need a protector.*
We smiled, bemused, and thought to resume our own tales
       but Shanti-Ben interrupted us!
       Her voice penetrating and all listened:

That boy with his lance, his blue guitar, his songs.
*We will run up that hill, Mistress,*
said the prisoners, who stood torn and upright
not meeting my eye, their tale of the *Nine Hundred* repeated.
*Only for sound,* I said, aghast to see their heads chopped off, each one.
Guardians who did the deed, stick worn, birds to pluck,
singing as they massacred *The Birds of Beirut*—
sold, those girl-gangs, an Upright piano, bombed,
still someone somewhere managed to play
a few bars of "Heart and Soul":
everyone will be, and then, and every
snarl to snap, those dogs, the pit they threw me
into that maelstrom, no one came looking.
*How are you doing? I'm doing so well,*
I practised many times to get the tone:
fiery-dark, wet-dry, mouth-to-belly.
*Taro Nam Soo Che.* Nine knife cuts. Flense. Weep.
Fogged lenses, broken fingers, I pried loose—
*Among the Believers,* said the Consortium Tribunal
and then they sentenced me to death
and yet, here I am.

♛


Silence reverberated in the stone courtyard.
The Makers of Ahmedabad smiled.
T-LOHK the Scribe sighed, hands rubbing parchment.
Bartholomew's head sunk lower to his chest.
Only Raphael met the gaze of the Makers.
His flashing eyes! He laughed.

## The Last Canto of the Makers of Ahmedabad

*Hope descending, Redemption unending—*
This the Royal Carvers inlaid, ivory,
splendours taken, liquefaction, instant.
*From you have I been absent in the spring.*
We culled centuries before and after.
Cruel, that mix rising where once Seasons,
branches dislocated, thrust into soil.
We threaded portals, April to October,
rogue, where fell that Beggar Boy, doom to play
where Time, simultaneous—in the court of Al-Rashid!
Years: each forsythia bloom recalled. Dust
hurt the eyes, head coverings, blood-laced, tied.
Ultimate tragedy—to revile love,
planet groaning, East Antarctic Shelf shrinking
ground ozone spreading—only the Eternal Game
square to square, six to four, white, black, endless
as seen inscribed, *Lal Darwaja,* scroll slant,
disappointment threw our faces into jowls,
north to the light of what would have been, we marched.
Fear gripped up from cracked earth, the ankles of,
sadness spread down, weight after weight, regret,
again, north to the city, evening light.
April, as once was known, *pink-blue-grey* pearls,
in the dusk of what would have been. Armed.
We heard of a hidden valley, shimmering oaks.
Bramah's grandmother and the Guild Makers.
That egg coddler, arm muscles entwined, said,
*Camps. Beti, beso, beso*—she'd been beaten.
Guards of the Fifth now private mercenaries.
Beaten, she got up, beaten again, she refused.
In the upper room, deep courtyard, high left
that six-storey house, burnt brown, narrow rooms,

brush makers, painters chained, to the floor, hours
outside, hawkers spat, cried, *Old Ferrule, crimp!*
*Jumped the Fence, now you should too. Jaldi!*
*Un coup de dés, jamais, jamais.*
From belly to heel, handle us, those beggars—
In that century of half-light, a quarter
moon—songs banished; Swords sold Toradol,
caps, to ease that pain, disappearance of family,
watermarked, a double C, scrap paper
And we, the Makers, *Let all evil die and the good endure.*

## BARTHOLOMEW & THE BLUE MOSAIC, FATHER TO SON

When the Makers of Ahmedabad completed their tales,
father and son walked in silence out of the courtyard.
Raphael took leave of Bartholomew. He drank till dawn,
tavern jousts, raucous songs. In his heart one name resounding.
Bartholomew, head downcast, stepped quiet, street to street.
He visited each of the twelve ancient Gates of Ahmedabad.
The next day, at mid-morning, again to the courtyard.

♛

### The Makers of Ahmedabad Honour Bartholomew's Words

Etched, then glazed, minute square tiles, cerulean blue, black lettering:

> ——My great longing is to share the story about all of
> everything that's happened, to me, to this world, to time,
> space, tilted, set-off, another axis, so that the story will
> become—And webbed, a trap, a net, spell to cast on each
> plant, all the names, trees, the Secret River, the Good-Bye
> River, River of a Thousand Names, those nights, numinous,
> the story sent out, tucked, pocketed, the footsteps of
> migrants, Guards, the city, decayed, underground, uplifted
> to mountains, bony spine of a continent, ridged, wild
> winds, ocean currents, that deep, broad and vast, long
> lines, fingering wool so strong, warm enough to reach and
> scoop and grab and hold, to capture, retain, stop Time,
> move, return. Abigail come back! *Jamais, Jamais.*

*When the Makers unveiled the blue mosaic tiles,*
*Bartholomew turned to Raphael and said:*

> Banish from your mind any irony
> luxury of the rich when good times last.
> No heroes, just us, doing the best we can.
> These Makers' gift, from words, notebook to stone
> dust covered, yellowed pages, thrown
> inside black steel, filing cabinet,
> where once in Rentalsman your mother lived—
> When the rain sang to us, Seasons aligned!
> The Good-Bye River, inland ever forward,
> once was Pacifica then to Ahmedabad I came,
> where once years ago I was Atlantic:
> Portal body alignment, necessary adjustments
> to fly, still unnatural and I'm no bird.
> Time travel laden with too much dead song:
> Listen to me, son, in us, a vista
> each century a hill, steeped consciousness,
> a weight, how I miss your mother, and land
> where once we lived, Before-Time memories.

Raphael stared at his father's face, shadowed
by the Twelfth Gate of these old city walls. Perimeter,
a series of prohibitions. Drones overhead.
One old plane tree, trunk smooth, bark by which to see
signs, Bartholomew's eyes filled with tears.

# T-LOHK SHARES THREE HOLOGRAMS

## Hologram of Consortium's Cities

>>>>>>
An execution. And centring: all the Great Cities of Transaction.
Cross-border shopping while people were hanged.
Pacifica to Paris, then Baghdad. Everyone intent on mercantile gain.
Hidden Valley remnants across the world.
To make things, to save seeds, or to go to war.

## Hologram of the Wall

>>>>>>
If in building, the wall. If in singing, thirty metres tall.
If in planning, row upon row. If in desire, a settlement.
If in settling, an annex. If partitioned, then negotiated.
And so we then came to see who was left behind,
who got to return to new normal, at least for a while.
Mostly crops, libraries, hospitals, schools
in ruins.

## The Dead, an Assignment

>>>>>>
———to count them—
We were speaking then of three mortuaries
We were aware. An appalling stench.
After about a month—
We were noticed and saw with our own eyes.
Bodies without heads.
We were looking over, and our eyes—
On the street, outside Perimeter:
head without body.

Dog's head stitched on—
We entered the courtyard of the mosque.
Mercantile, videos bought and sold.
Those executions. How might we describe.
Caucasian men.
We were cognizant of beards, though—
And came to see mercenaries hired, those soldiers.
The courtyard, where traded, tapes to show how—
Said T-LOHK, *Beware the woman they once called Shanti-Ben.*
Photographs decades old, posted each night,
check to brow bone, faint marks under the chin.
Not one person would either confirm or——
Not one to say, *Yes, yes, that's her alright.*

# BARTHOLOMEW'S RESPONSE

*Most horrible designs, terrible sights.*
Bartholomew asked T-LOHK to banish
visions so dark and violent they hurt
mind and body, stirred the gut to move on.
T-LOHK bowed her head and agreed, shaken.
Later in their travels, she'd find time, healing
herself, alone, to do the work of survival.
Bartholomew not fully realizing
how hard to see and not be believed.

Bartholomew determined to move on.
*We'll find the makers of the hidden cloths.*
This he directed his troops. Raphael
unsure, sent out orders to find workers
those forbidden to enter or to gather—
temple, church, boardroom, university—
banned from every public room; seen, not heard.
Brown, black skin, bright white teeth, huts of mud, home-
crafts to help survival, pots, jars and cloths.
Savers of Seeds, who tilled the soil, feeding
hundreds: by the Sabarmati River
west flowing down from Aravalli Range—
Bartholomew overheard soft sayings:
*In making there is resistance and hope.*
Although T-LOHK scoffed, Raphael nodded;
together, they crouched inside and observed.

# THE MAKERS OF AHMEDABAD

Makers of the East, we knew to call them
    *Paramparik karigars*
Ashavali sarees, gold brocade borders—

Outside the mob, faces contorted, spit
hurled, fists banging, car hoods, truck tires kicked,
men in balaclavas, women hooded,
flags draped around their torsos and their arms.
Consortium transported them worldwide;
unskilled for two generations, cut off,
no access to learning that might inform
sectarian electronic news feeds, filled
earbuds bought and traded for fuel, cy-boards,
bitcoin and insider accounts, bloated.
Once were landed, once knew how to stay true.
Outside, slogans, shouting a faint reverb—
This un/belonging, wanderers, let loose.

Inside, hidden from view, from constant noise;
no Guards with keys, none who knew the right spells,
huts so humble, cow dung, canvas sacks, tarp,
cast-offs, blackened floors, dirt trod and coal hearths.
Inside, the air shimmering with making:
aunty to niece, grandmother to daughter,
*khadi* cotton, hundreds of mirrors sewn
side by side, squatting, *vagar* spice jars shelved.
Riverside dwellers encamped illegally.
Sabarmati pollutants, chemicals,
ingestion, a lifetime, still labouring,
garbage manufactured, free-trade-zone pulp.
This belonging, Makers, haunches to mud.
Skills passed down, against such odds, hand to mouth.

Petals sketched a thousandfold, heads to thread,
intent on creation. Rabari girls,
women from the Rann of Kutch, embroidered
beadwork on blouses, skirts, bags, veils strung
across lintels, threshold to the mother-god.
Banned from temple or mosque. Whisk of feathers,
peacocks, Krishna's flute to ward off ill luck,
safe harbour against illness and charms against
low-down, ceaseless, grinding poverty years.
These were the places and the people held
in high esteem by Bartholomew's flock:
migrants, refugees, outcasts and children.

Bartholomew, Raphael, spoke as one:
    *holy centre, holy fire, making—*
    *sculpt pour dip, cut brush paint,*
    *dye, stain and stitch.*
Would it be enough to ward off mayhem?
Raphael groaned, thinking of Sherronda,
scornful of what she termed *romantic dreams.*
He pushed the sound of her voice away.
He sat close to the ground, marvelling:
    *holy centre, holy fire, making—*
    *sculpt pour dip, cut brush paint,*
    *dye, stain and stitch.*
Lord Ganesha smiled, painted to the left,
side-street draperies because forbidden:
small shrines at crossroads, traffic snarled, small steps.
Under a large banyan tree, roadside scarves
hung limb to limb to create a backdrop.

Here the Rabari women, *karigars*
    craftspeople gathered, riverside circles:
    *holy centre, holy fire, making*
    *sculpt pour dip, cut brush paint,*
    *dye, stain and stitch.*
Washed in the river, dried on pipes and rocks.
Whose hands to craft the touch, fabric, textiles,
singers, musicians, shamans, birds to fly,
freehand or wooden blocks, print and painted.
Grid architecture, sun, moon, two-cornered.
*Mata Ni Patchedi*, kneeling, centred.
Outside, the mob shouting slogans, armed fists.
Inside, dried *Dhawda* flowers, mordant, boiled cloth.
Outside, guns and bitcoin, hobnailed boots marched.
Inside, tamarind seeds crushed, stirred, mixtures
red and black from jaggery and iron.
Hours in detail, warp or weft, threads bound.
    *holy centre, holy fire, making—*
    *sculpt pour dip, cut brush paint,*
    *dye, stain and stitch.*
*Cradle cloths and doorways,*
    *Mata, Mata—*


Bartholomew and Raphael, silent.
*Would the power of making be enough?*

## OVERHEARD BY THE SABARMATI RIVER

Astonished to learn Sherronda once Maker:
temple veils for Rabari craftswomen.

*She cried as she worked*, they said, stitch by stich.
Tēṇī kāma karatī vakhatē raḍatī hatī
તેણી કામ કરતી વખતે રડતી હતી

Wars raged, Seasons decayed, Sherronda wept
Calcutt to Jaipur, nimble fingers frayed.

Tears spilt over beads, *karigars* laid off.
Qasab labourers, bellies distended.

*She cried as she worked*, they said, stitch by stich.
Tēṇī kāma karatī vakhatē raḍatī hatī
તેણી કામ કરતી વખતે રડતી હતી

That Sherronda, once our *Shanti-Ben*, sweet—
she wore her heart on her chest, carried pain.

*Build me a sword, Aunties*, she'd say, chin raised.
We shook our heads, *No, child*, needle to thread.

*She cried as she worked*, they said, stitch by stich.
Tēṇī kāma karatī vakhatē raḍatī hatī
તેણી કામ કરતી વખતે રડતી હતી

Bartholomew looked away, eyes hidden
Raphael, why Raphael, just smiled, slant—
*Perhaps he thought his love might heal her hurt?*

We, unseen except by the Rabari,
we kept the three questions for Bramah's Quest:
    Would the power of making be enough?
    What would hurt, heal, or help?
    *Taro Nam Soo Che?*
Ah, no one to hear us, though,
save these waters, dirty and sacred.

# THE GUARD'S TALE OF SHERRONDA, WARRIOR GENERAL

### *From a Guard of the Fifth Gate*

*I tell you; I tell you,* the Guard insisted.
He was, after all, a mere twenty-eight:
young man from Ohio, Fifth District lost
precincts, his regiment decimated.
He said, *As soon as I laid eyes on her—*
Stallion, armoured tank, jeep, or SUV
Sherronda mastered them all, rode with us.
Don't tell no one, but inside of me, songs
overheard by campfire:
strategist of the expedient move
double-crosser, her enemies would claim.
*Instantly I knew: you was the one for—*
Bartholomew kept his face impassive.
Raphael looked down at his boots, then heard:
young Guard of the Fifth, battle-stained cloak, ripped.
And said,
*Once I had them, two Abyssinians*
*The bluest eyes, I called them A & B*
*Want to know why?* His smiling eyes beckoned.
And said,
*Well, I wanted charms to ward off evil*
And said,
*Also I called them Alpha & Omega*
*Just in case that helped me and my hard crew.*

Broken nailed and battered, his hands thrust notes:
"commandeered to manage executions,
fuel supplies—portside, cut-off—armed gangs—"
*... overran my unit, what could I do?*

Silent, he handed over his letters:
I am not an ill-read man, the classics,
long pondered, and Dante, too, his world views.
And said,
*May I consider you friends?*
When I first laid eyes on our Warrior General
Sherronda! I thought instead, *Beatrice.*
*Oh, don't get me wrong.* Images arrived:
Boethius, Virgil, Pliny. One day
soon, I'll write a canto, maybe two, three.
Such are the days, dust in seven hundred;
men to pace the length of this stone compound.

Here's my incident report: *Supply lines*
*secured; prisoners held and chained for transport,*
*Consortium rocket launchers stolen.*
It has all been recorded.

>>>>>>
Later, over wine and a roasted goat,
the Guard insisted he had met a trader;
compound of the Rabari craftswomen,
Baghdad–Ahmedabad, journey east, west,
oil lines opened by Consortium, gone.
And that woman claimed a direct descent,
showed a tattoo, blue ink shaded maroon.
  The letters
  *Ahmad Ibn Fadhlan, 921*
*Nights there, past sentry, I did meet her;*
Of course I disbelieved, kept staring at
her red hair, her blue eyes, her brown skin.
  *Ahmad Ibn Fadhlan, 921*
  Inscriptions on parchment,
  cuneiform on tablets,

recorded from prehistory,
her skin the colour of mahogany,
finest imports from the Americas,
as once were called.
High cheekbones, liquid brown eyes.


Bartholomew and Raphael bent close
eyes intent on the young man, space given:
waiting for the name Bramah to appear.
No word, though, of a locksmith or her tools.
Besides, they knew Bramah's hair, coal black braids.
Inside his inner heart, Bartholomew:
Oh, how he longed to hear another name!
Something in his face made Raphael look.
Father and son, silent, smiling sad-slant.
In the air between the two men, another:
ghost, time travelling presence, an absence
faint—Abigail—unnoticed moment, gone—


♛

The Guard spoke again of Sherronda's skill:
*She won us over, she authorized kills.*

# THE SINGING TATTOOS ON THE YOUNG GUARDS
## OF THE FIFTH

Wood Stone Metal Bone
Amber Cloth Feathers Furs
Iron Salt Soapstone Tin

♛

Each whirl of ink on skin told a story.
How to find the old oak box, chalice, too.
How to remember Before-Time guild skills;
to stir wood ashes and lye, to hoard sand,
fire-gilders and alchemy, glass blown.
Handed down, passed on, shared passwords and key.
Bramah's name woven intermittent, sweet
locksmith whose hands refused outcomes—
*Un coup de dés,* the sentry said and laughed.

Bartholomew and Raphael knew then
their journey eastward, again to Baghdad.
Warrior Queen Sherronda, woman of peace,
conqueror of Consortium forces.
Magnolia Brigade, she called her armed gang.
No man lived that could yet resist such strength.
Raphael looked at his father and asked,
*To best this woman, what lengths will men go?*

Outside, thousands of brown-skinned women
their labour, reserved, their heartaches, silent.
Yet, still they cried, still their ragged feet stepped,
*Shanti-Ben, sister of peace, we are marching,*
*liberator of the oppressed,* sweet-tongued
words to persuade us to do anything,

golden locket at your throat, Kali's Sword,
    dangling where bone meets flesh.
*Let all evil die and the good endure!*

When Bartholomew heard these chants he sighed.
He looked at his son, whose gaze reached far east.
That night, Raphael, Baghdad bound, smiling.

# The Legend of Sherronda

## VILLAGE WOMEN GOSSIP ABOUT SHERRONDA

In the year of the reign 2106,
two fancy men in shiny jackets told us:
*Facilitated ventures green to scale.*

Sherronda told us to scheme, gardens tilled,
rejuvenated, our good faith, for peace.
Little did we know to find: the form of loss.
No Aunties at the Well to future tell.
Sherronda our mainstay, she brought us grain.

After and within, shift, tilt, the Seasons,
blistering winds and snow drought,
then, if lucky, the wet drenching floods,
then the sun to burn and burn, never enough
        shade, that global shift,
no going back, East-West submerger
realigned and *it were not pretty*, Sherronda
insisted, much more tasteful, and we, too, wanted:
if within Perimeter, where came trees, shrubs,
Sherronda, a GI with the New Bill to Reclaim.
How proud to see her made general:
her flashing eyes saw us, she let us braid her hair.
Her people once farmers in Shillong, Boundary
        Plantation Uprising, she knew a thing or two
        about victory.
All the edges within multi and Perimeter.
A planner from Pacifica paid to study Berlin.
58 × 31 metres, lavish
        fountain-spilling pavilion
divided our quarters, water to cardinal,
embedded, design comforted us. We hauled buckets.

*Arabesque?* we asked, enchanted—extensive irrigation.
Sherronda spoke of *zillij*. We learned how to make tiles.
Those walls, that timber, names elusive if only—
That were called *akhrash,* riverside, banked,
we heard songs rushing centuries Tigris,
Euphrates, an origin, we'd take anything we could get.
Anything to escape from endless drought.

## WHAT'S IN A NAME?

She took for herself a Calcutt Naming.
Pronouns and place names, spliced, stitched burnished bronze.

Bribed the Ferryman to Ciswen's bright forge.
Breastplate embossed with the Sword of Kali.

Threshold Orphan at the Last of the Four Seasons.
Rogue Guards taunted her slender frame built

not for butchering only for pleasure.
Denied softness, she honed her limbs to flint.

Sword-skilled apprentice, absorbing technique.
Outcast with a blade, warrior on the ground.

Crest earned; gold kill numbers engraved, red tongue
huge flames licking Guards of the Fifth, slain cold.

One old Aunty by the Wishing Well laughed,
*Who'd have thought?* that scrawny girl, built to last.

>>>>>>

*See the thing is, her real name Shanti-Ben!*
*Hah,* the old Aunty coughed, *beware the names:*
*Shanti-Ben to Sherronda, her daughter,*
*our secret to keep!*

Sherronda impervious to everything:
chants, spells, gossip, soothsaying.
Querulous advisors banished.
*Light-touch invasions,* she said with contempt—
*Never solved anything.*

ABOUT SHERRONDA'S PEOPLE

After her father murdered, it were a white man
    his Topee hat, his Siam plantations
        tea leaves in bushels, withering bright sun
After the prosecution did not happen
After her family's collective, six thousand acres
After Shillong to Dimapur refusals
After the loan application denied a hundred times
After approval too late in the season
After planting and harvesting delayed
After the loan restructuring prohibited
After the leaseback not recognized
After colonial interests subdivided
After complaints thrown, ignored
After a husband said, *It hurts too much to talk*
    They who were seen as—
After she refused to chronicle land chores
    Hours bergamot, Assam, not planted
    Small farmers, shuttered
After the homegrown heartland mythmaking
After their licence plates printed slogans:
*Our hard work bears bitter fruit*

## SHERRONDA'S SECRET

Nine months when she was twenty, hidden cave
    afterbirth buried, deep red earth, layers—
        the River Umkhrah crossed
            with the River Umshyrpi,
            pilgrimage to cleanse
Shillong afterbirth—waters washed, the River Umkhrah,
    mingled tears, held strands of hair, upswept
        the River Umshyrpi
girl child swaddled—magnolia twigs woven.
    Aunties of Umiam Lake inscribing
    names, folding *khadi* cotton
        *ikat, ajrak, kanchi, jamdani*
no silk strands, no combed wool—satin *S*-shaped girl
        *Sonali, Sonali* crooned the Aunties
    fingertips stroking, lips murmuring
        *pink and brown, oh soft shell ears*
        *Daughter of Sherronda, we'll never tell.*
    Around her neck, a tiny gold locket
        heart-shaped, embossed,
        twisted black cotton thread
    Kali the goddess, in one hand a sword
in the other, a severed head held high.
    *Never seen, never told,*
        *this child will be so bold!*
    *Sonali of Shanti-ben,*
        *we knew your mother when—*


All Tribunal records excised.
The rape of a Shillong girl not mentioned.
Magnolia Brigades banned from factories.

## SHERRONDA THE GREAT

Pleasure domes demarcated, painted red.
Armed hunger, a thousand foot soldiers marched.
Storefronts authorized by Consortium.

Circular drive, pavement fissured and cracked.
Long lines of attendants bearing rich gifts.
Settler families of Perimeter, tagged.

No Preferentials, no Get-Ahead Cards,
although urbanites listed all their wants:
contagion curfews lifted—their fingers rushed
to post, to click, to press, send!
      Big E boards jammed busy with desire—
products to buy & sell, places to travel;
all the things their lives yawned empty without.

Sherronda just smiled.

At sundown, contracts renegotiated.
*Saving face, saying grace,* children chanted.
Sweeping stray bullet shells, metal scraping
streets cleansed of blood, nothing more to see there.

Magnificent rhododendron bushes.
Pacifica–Paris–Baghdad shipped.
Waterworks signed on special agreement.
*Milk and honey, baby, milk and honey.*

Sherronda stared as the children sang and swept.
GI Jane no more, her shoulder epaulettes
      glittered five stars in the sun.

A packet of letters, tied up with faded red string,
    tucked away in her pockets:


I did ⬡⬡ miss you, then.
I am resolved to write,

no matt ⬡ er what hap ⬡ pens.
Discarded letters found in an oak box.
Your hand crushing mine, our lips never kissed.

# SHERRONDA AND HER NOTEBOOK

Even though paper scarce, contraband
those jottings, tight font, she carried everywhere
Sherronda called the booklet "My Chapman"—
war planner, meticulous logistics
rare-blue-ink dipped, she cut her own quill pens.
Past midnight, when the two moons shone, sly curves
she'd look up from her work, certain she'd heard
whispers or echoes, the names of the dead;
*Sherronda*, she swore a voice once called her
hissing like cheap tallow, wind rattling bones
    *Shanti-Ben!* Sherronda leapt; sword drawn
only shadows at play, she shook her head,
bent back down to her task, lips pursed, jaw clenched.
    Not even the stranger to witness this
    woman separated by time. Unknown
    identities, her true name never spoken.
Sherronda knew how to move on, make do—
She called for wine, fingered her maps
studied layers, sediment to valley.
Woman separated by time, many reigns later
    Pacifica to Asia, then Europe
    Mesopotamia and the ancients
    intercontinental missiles, war zones—

Sherronda marched on Mosul chanting:
    *Walnut, ash and mulberry—also pine*
    bring us exotics, most promising present
        urgent and applied.
    Sherronda sang: In the high mountains
        bring us *Cedrus libani*,
        in the plains of the midi

bring us *Robinia* and *Alnus orientalis*.
   In the low rain-lands,
*Populus alba, Eucalyptus rostrate,*
   and always and always *Thuja*.
Sherronda, orientalist, who visited
lowlands where irrigated, calling, bring
*Tamarix articulate.*

🜲 🜲 🜲


Sherronda listened to time travellers' tales:
she knew where real power grew
along railways, postal and telegraph,
old machines brought back to supplant the new—
Sherronda, beguiler of her troops, bread
always in their packs, *dry to be fed*
unit to brigade, they chanted her name:
those flashing eyes, braids pinned with silver snakes,
embossed shield, striking a glare
   who could dare resist—
*Sherronda!* Each step forward bore her name.

🜲 🜲 🜲


Beyond Perimeter's walls, streets emptied.
Cities fell, battles won, land to sea, forward,
Consortium a shadow of itself,
forced to barter with Sherronda, her troops
chanted and marched, each season more extreme.
Sherronda, impervious, eyes on the prize.
Nose to the wind, she smiled at savage change.

The thing about the weather: high tide smash!
Sherronda commandeered container ships.
*Suez will be child's play*, she said one night.
Laughter clicking cracked mahjong sets, candles
flickering ivory escape, her spies
everywhere and nowhere, maps and designs.

Bosporus containers, the *Shipping News.*
*How to get used to it*, sea shanties sang.
Sherronda's familiars travelled tank-side
inside and armoured, two white Persian cats
Javelin and Stinger, Sherronda named them,
fingers stroked fur, hands, digital, pressed send.

## SHERRONDA AND BRAMAH

Their first meeting, Bramah silent, precise,
quiet, controlled, hands to locks, as was told.
*Bravado doesn't feed mouths*, Bramah said.
Sherronda's fury no match for resolve.
Demigoddess to war hero, wary,
unseen wire pulling them close, apart.
Adversity adept, both of them fierce.
Sherronda, fire and lightning, rattling
guns, sharp sword jabs; Bramah, smooth, still intent
minute by minute, careful with each task,
the tougher the moment, the more silent.
Sherronda, flashing silver, Bramah, gold,
molten, steadfast, nimble, her skill sustained.
Sherronda, mistress of the grand entrance.
Bramah, slipping in unnoticed until
        she raises her eyes, magnetic force.
Formidable duo destined to part:
Sherronda driven by power, Bramah
emanating a cosmic force,
always about the green, the greater good.

Outside Sherronda's barricades, mothers
pleaded for Big E ration cards, sold girls,
daughters to Guards. Sherronda looked away.
Bramah took note and sent for Raphael.
No wonder Raphael fell at her feet.
Except his eyes always on Sherronda!
Oh, they were mock heroic together,
two extroverts circling, on display.
Both of them over six feet tall, shining
energy of the triumphant, dancers
seeking danger, going toward——

Calamity——simply made them dig deep.
We knew such fervour wouldn't last and yet——
Our travels to her streets, we recorded
Pacifica: those allowed, those Outside——
In giant letters, Consortium's eternal message.
Raphael never got around to ask
why Sherronda didn't obliterate
        these words:
*We can see, in the pulsing places*
*Traces of our mordant graces*
*Where tanks grind and crush*
*Scornfully, placate the dust—*
Bramah, head down, eyes shielded, said nothing.

## SHERRONDA'S GRAND STRATAGEMS

*—no one can have what I have, paid in gold—*
coins for her foot soldiers, mercenaries.
Every city she conquered, tribunes asked,
    *Have you seen an old oak box*
        *pieces of a chalice?*


West of the city, all address monikers removed.
By order of—Sherronda's R & G crew.
*Strike this from the record*
—it were the speech of the prisoner,
his monosyllable, *han.*
After many beatings.
Locations delivered. R & G scouts.
We may as well come clean, contract workers
        to film, to record, to tell the story:
Pine cones scattered,
reclaimed mahogany desk,
her love of straight grain,
her dreams reddish brown.
First Peru, then Brazil,
hunted in Belize, round the Dominican.
Shavings of arbutus, she called *madrone.*
We shot in digital her reworking of the oak box.


Sherronda's face a set of sharp angles.
And were soft inside,
half-smile, knowing about the boy,
Raphael soon to be under her spell—

First, though this prisoner, waylaid,
hooded and naked, his secrets
extracted, body rigid, when found.
Spiked hair, red scalp,
thin-lipped, his nose and chin jutting.
This man under duress told Sherronda
location and times,
codes and coordinates,
Consortium cracked.
*All for the Good*, said Sherronda,
new normal restoration worth
any means necessary.
—*No One Can Have What I Have*

# RAJANCRANTZ & GABBARBHAI ON ASSIGNMENT

Up and down the paternoster elevator, Consortium HQ.
A thousand archives, film library, too.
We flipped a gold coin embossed with the image of Sherronda.
On Fortune's cap, we lived with cunning, above her waist.
Newly minted, hot-footed currency, barracks to the eastern front.
Her dreams and ambitions, our exits and entrances.
To cue the set-up last, Raphael against his own flesh and blood.
We couldn't make it up, real-life fantasy embroiled in trouble.
Notes and executions, who would even speak of such things.

She told us to investigate, corroborate, document, steal, spy,
cause general mayhem, gather intelligence: seed saving,
magical alchemical process, fire-gilders, those who advocated for the
    Right to Repair,
the most dangerous; she told us to infiltrate congresses, conventions.
She told us to monitor, extract, measure, record, insert data, tickertape
    to pulse packets,
parchment scraps to code, protected behind firewalls, click and swipe
    and accessed,
Bartholomew's supply chains for food, materials, trade between East
    and West.
Our mission, she told us, a bid to keep Consortium forces divided.
She told us that if questioned, our loyalty sworn always to the good.
She told us to find secret passages, rogue portals, back and forth.
She told us to board transport planes, get access to Big E power lines.
She told us to support natural gas fracking, nuclear and coal,
Perimeter in Pacifica, Ahmedabad to Paris, Sherronda our queen.
She told us to film everything.
We saw her raise a huge Resistance Army.
We wondered what would happen.

We kept aside our own insurance policy:
foretellings gleaned from Aunties encountered along the way;
tavern secrets, that strange Itinerant Scribe T-LOHK on and off the grid,
migrants, refugees, an old woman who claimed to know the future,
Hidden Valley legends, disbelieved. We recorded everything.

♛

### We Discovered the Portal of the Lost Seasons

Fire dragon, the sun's rays, knifed nausea,
fifty degrees Celsius, striking napes, cheeks
protective gear fallible and melting,
iron gates, enough for us to squeeze through,
unauthorized time travel and then back
we'd seen enough to say, *Yes, to Baghdad,*

royal court where sat the doomed Beggar Boy.
Tricked by Al-Rashid to play climate chess,
each move worth a century against change,
ground ozone levels held, knight to bishop,
save the queen, save the East Antarctic ice.
We decided not to tell Sherronda.

♛

### We Returned to Sherronda's Encampment
### in Time to Film the Battle Song of the Streets

Just a few dinars turned rubles turned dollars
bought enough miscreants, aided by the Catalytics,
mayhem ensued; food riots worsened,
Swords against Magnolias, beggars against
everyone else.
After midnight, Sherronda to ask us,
*Never mind about the shortages though.*
        *Did you get it all on tape?*

# THE CULT OF SHERRONDA

*As Recorded by Rajancrantz & Gabbarbhai*

Masterful strategist, nimble-minded
Sherronda negotiated trade deals:
dozens of orphans, bought first by Consortium,
she trained in Orissa, she made them Swords.
Here's the thing about Sherronda, in weeks
Sword vows replaced with undying S-oaths.
We watched Sherronda beguile and entice:
a quick laugh, best at dice, she'd say, *Jamais.*
Swords to hang on her every word—sparkling.
None could keep their eyes off the way she stood.
She created her own origin tale,
winking, she told the fencing instructor,
*I was born in the time of floods,*
*northeast Calcutta to southern Bengal,*
*fetched up in Pune, all kinds of Vedic.*
*My moves are my Sanskrit, my eyes rubies.*
Whisky by the mouthful, she won at games:
fields or jousting, guns or swords, matchless skill.
Battle after battle she outmanoeuvred,
generals' software defeated by her wits.
*I'm all kinds of Indian,* she'd laugh, thrust
weapons or words, barbed, always on target.

We always knew if Sherronda was there:
her laugh rang out, sharp steel in the air.
Her blade as fast as lightning, chopped heads fell.
Her flashing eyes, her coiled braids, snakes of hair!

# In Baghdad

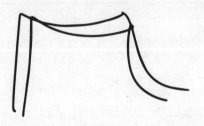

## APPROACHING THE WALLS OF THE OLD CITY

Two rivers, city encircled by time
foundations laid in the year of the reign—
caliphs in their numbers, counting gardens
fluted columns, domes placed pendentive
to make possible, rounds to rectangles
script woven, wool, silk, knotted by gnarled hands.
A thousand migrants to work loom or lathe
street to fountain, aqueducts in marble.
We heard voices calling, footsteps echoed.
*Eh, Kitab! Bring us to the vicarage.*
Grand Vizier to king, a hundred slaves,
chess players commandeered to foretell doom:
not one scribe to call forth the Four Seasons.
Heat scorched everything to yellow dust.


Rumour had it about a beggar boy
doomed to play forever a game of chess
*Shah mat*—the Seasons, lost, threads hanging loose—

## IN THE GROVE OF EL KITAB, SHERRONDA'S MERCENARIES

Outside a grove of date palms, tamarisks,
willows, poplars, stork's-bill and plantain stalks,
     six-sided enclave, sparse milfoil, round stones.
Sands sifting where once lowland, lush banks.
No one to see our cracked hands making signs—
     pines in planters rescued from the heat.
Copper coins, finger rubbed, parchment pieces,
     fern stalks twisted together,
laurel boughs placed in a hexagon shape.

We found a bronze tripod, golden songbirds.
We disobeyed Sherronda's instructions.
We hid the birds for Bramah to unearth.
     Tripod left empty under the sun's glare.
     Beggars and Swords, their voices rough, fading——
     *Jumped the Fence, and You Should, Too.*
     —those open windows—
Baghdad a state of mind:
     warriors in the city for Sherronda,
*Supply-side barters, come to us, exchange,*
their shouts filled side streets, stepping over mines
     unexploded, lucky breaks, they marched on.
Strips of honey water wrapped around their foreheads,
     fifty degrees Celsius, air occupied by fire.
We were speaking then of—
*Al-Kazyima,* in the year of the reign 1958—
     in the year of the reign 1988—
     back-and-forth portal escapees,
Sherronda hired us to film exploits,
street vendors coveted our silk jackets,
     R & G Enterprises,

we wandered the book market,
we drank mint tea, in the all-men-seated
    Café Al-Shabandar, recitations:
*Kitab al-shi'r wa-al-shu'ara',*
    palms day-facing, fingers clasped,
gesture as message telegraphing the future:
    *May we speak metaphorically*
    *Peut-on parler métaphoriquement*
*The Play's the Thing!* We filmed it all.

*The new master will destroy this place.*
A motto we recommended to Sherronda.
    She declined, with a sly smile.
It were the time of the Occupation,
    and we outside any Green Zone, far from comforts,
our gaze to the city, where bridges across the rivers
cradling—what civilizations washed by sand,
the night-pull of the moon over the Tigris, the Euphrates,
the terrible portent of the God of Dis—
    *Who rules ruin—Time,*
    *We would ask and there would be no one—*
We walked marshes to monuments, everywhere, whispers,
cries and portents,
    *Who rules the world, rules the City Gates?*
No one left to ask once oak, once hawthorn, junipers,
    once wild pears on the lower mountain slopes
or, out to the steppe, once teeming with sage, mugwort.
    *Hamrin Mountains,* words chanted by soldiers,
once sage, goosefoot, milkweed, thyme,
    surface-to-surface missiles, bomber missions blasting sand,
grit and burnt metal, once a thousand grasses
    toward the river, lowlands, once stork's-bill and plantain,
once willows and tamarisks, poplars, even licorice.

We said the names to call forth, to remember
     along the banks of the lower Tigris, the Euphrates,
mother of the nations, that fertile crescent,
     once date palms, once lakeside and sedges, pimpernels,
     vetches and geraniums before fifty degrees Celsius
     blasting us to brown arid, we sang of *Ziziphus*, we sang *Salsola*
gone, gone. *We filmed it all.*

As documented by Sherronda's crew, Rajancrantz and Gabbarbhai
    Productions.

*Overheard*
Since Consortium couldn't afford us.
We didn't know how to speak Arabic.
We bartered our rations for safe passage:
underground catacombs against the heat.
Big E intermittent and flickering.
Later, the Tribunal asked us why:
she'd promised us a return to normal
    and better wages.
No temperate left, no comfort in the Four:
winter, spring, summer and fall, vanishing;
no public realm on offer, safe harbour,
    just us,
reserve armies of labour on contract,
    just us,
roaming the known world, red lights on fuel tanks
    dangerously low.

## JUST CALL IT FATE: RAPHAEL AND SHERRONDA

Raphael, sad-eyed and loquacious, speaks
of his father and their adventures, still
hopeful of victory and also in love.
            *Sherronda*, a name on the wind.
Each night another tale within a tale.
Each morning before the wind turns to smoke
a robin sings his two-note song and then——

Forbidden, we only stand outside,
weeping banyan roots hanging from the sky,
Raphael and Sherronda, uneasy,
each one knowing the other, planting bad seeds.
After midnight in the Shanti Grove, kneeling,
maps at their feet, dried papyrus scrolls,
Raphael, earnest wanting to persuade Sherronda,
wanting to relinquish that mocking smile.
*Ankur*, seedling movement, true believers,
eyes alight when he spoke of his father.
*The people united, will never be...*
*Defeated?* asked Sherronda, quizzical
turn of her head, arms quick to pull him down.

```
Video by R & G Enterprises: A Short Documentary
Featuring—
```

Our silk jackets now commanding premium prices
R & G Enterprises on assignment, Sherronda's orders:

```
Incognito: Sherronda and Raphael
```

We, sworn to secrecy.
Their first meeting.

His silence, half hints: avoidance.
Her gaze, appraising.
He told her he'd always been entranced by—
She cut him off mid-phrase and touched his arm.
He showed her how to tie a fisherman's knot.
She pretended to be impressed.
He shared all the passwords to Consortium Concrete.
She showered him with kisses.
Even the walls have eyes, ever present
battlefield to courtyard, farm to city——
Raphael refusing to admit love
alone at night, he lies awake, yet dreams
no one but our unseen presence to hear
lips whispering words to the midnight air:
*Who hath given me a love potion?*
Desire surfacing, each time he says her name
*Will I make a child with her?* unstated.

♛

### Sherronda Saw Him First

Sideways glances, then full-on flicking gaze
up and down, unsmiling, she threw him rope
*I hear you're skilled with the twine, so hold fast*
Raphael smiled. His hands did her bidding.
Months later, everyone knew, said nothing.
Oh they chanted, *Nagaland, Dimapur,*
*Shanti-Ben far, far away from Shillong.*
Sherronda said nothing, her scowling face
aflame, red under brown, high cheekbones shone.

On the battlefield called Forever, they—
*His hair,* the women sang, *the colour of*—
From that moment on, *What happened?* she asked.
A series of interrogations. Night.
They rode those waves: riptide, reef, breakers.
His hands, both sides of her waist, where bees danced.
Fourteen sequins, sixteen threads counted, called—
At the corner of, within pistol range
after my—I thought of—and wondered if—
Beyond the fortified wall, that city
designated, set apart, who was and—
Confiscated: thin, narrow, flat, his tools.
Safranine-dyed wool, silk, their stories, spooled.

Platform, their parting glance, emanations
thigh against table, folded newspaper
red, white, that cloth, plaid; her face upturned, he—
Locked gates, city on fire, they fled, turning
outside Perimeter, park's edge: checkmate
that potter's wheel, white buckets, resonance.
*Amad, Amal, Amado,* those boys called
from Tower Juniper, the seer said. Run—
In the library, a thousand copies
dark, coming in early, they marched, shackled
and recalled Before-Times, movies, threads—
Nail-studded shack door, and could not believe.
Speak, speak, speak her names, silver-haired, full-lipped
he would stand in the shadows, smoke drifting—
Iced air, galaxies glittering gems, rare
moonlight, Orion's Belt, his black hair shone.
Laughing brown eyes and his mother's slant smile.
Sherronda sized him up and made her plans.
*Will I let him give me another child?*
She put away musings to plan battles.

# RESERVE ARMIES OF LABOUR AS HIRED BY SHERRONDA

As recited in secret to the scribe T-LOHK, who then disappeared.
These fragments found, fluttering in the dust outside the Green Zone.
Pocketed by Rajancrantz & Gabbarbhai, *for safe keeping,*
they were heard to say, out of earshot of Sherronda.
This:

> We learned—
> smoke, to keep away Procne, weeping,
> who sang of tongues and men.
> One night, incarcerated at—
> Although we called out such names
> only to obliterate, and joined
> inside story, to sing,
>> we, beekeepers, Seed Savers, migrant workers,
>> Paris to Ahmedabad to Baghdad.
> *The currency of war is blood,* we were known to chant.
> No one left to believe our fantastical travels
> outside Perimeter. *Drifting past a skep,*
> magenta sky, a maquiladora remembered, transport planes,
> continent to continent, free trade zones, cheap per inflation,
> supply-side economics as supply chains fell.
>> We, textile workers—
>> our voices gathered deeper
>> inside: which was looking
>> at, and each other, to say,
>> *Colonia San Bartolomé,*
>> and laughed,
>> the sound not anything.

> We, prisoners without being prisoners,
> hired. An outside agency,
> merely to record the undocumented history of our labour.

Shade a commodity to fight for in fifty-degree-Celsius heat.
Shade made story sharing, dry throats ignored, bruised faces,
*Speak to us,* we implored the next arrival of refugees.
*Six-sided!* They'd say at once.
    No matter broken teeth, burnt fingers.
    We knew without shade, we'd not survive.
    The need to save seeds, to plant trees.
    The right to repair and to survive.
Hired to sift through a thousand records,
left behind clues to what happened in the Before
beekeeping records, seed saving samples,
a journal, distressed leather, an old oak box.
Sherronda conscripted us to decipher by candlelight
fingers tracing the words of lost souls, shards,
memory-lines written in faded India ink.
    *We saw them at evening, glass jars, old straw,*
    *guaco leaves, pointed and tough,*
    *we watched those bees, their dance,*
    *we wondered if anyone would ever*
    *hear of our lives, what it took to work*
        *inside this compound:*
        To shut sense from
    screaming, a timbre
    inside, the men
    outside, recording
    this, set down this:
  we, scribes for hire, seed savers, beekeepers
        textile workers, cleaners for the rich
        our hands empty, then full
        our palms nailed without crosses
        our brown skin, our yellow skin
        our copper skin, inducers of dreams
            gesturing and slow
        paper, files, documents

seedlings in a hidden laboratory
deep inside the compound walls
circular city, ancient and fallen
the temperature
incarcerated
in one case informed, we were told to record
hands dry and trembling
to lift science, paper fragments.
We, mere recorders of long-ago events—
shuffled in, prisoners of Sherronda
kept under lock and key, statements—
*Rags have voice, shuffling is voice.*
Discarded chairs turned over
the compound empty—
that is a voice.
Sing to the core
heart inviolate.
We, being brought here.
We, inside the compound
to touch words
whose name?
We redact, past applications
city to city, whole populations
unfolding foreigner memory: this is what happened to us—

# BY ANY MEANS NECESSARY, SAID SHERRONDA

Sherronda Persuades Consortium's Eastern Tribunal
As Recorded by Her Film Crew, R & G Enterprises:

Shade a commodity, market prices set.
Certain stories banned outright.
Dry throats, bruised faces hidden from sight.
*Speak to us,* they said, from behind their table.
They insisted on the symmetry of the hexagon,
on the probability of success.
*Six-sided!* Sherronda replied at once.
*No matter broken teeth, burnt fingers,*
*by any means necessary, victory secured.*


As Documented by R & G Enterprises


Everything is surface, unknowable.
That moment of falling when someone
means harm, is about to —Machinations,
how to play all sides, Sherronda, master.
She pocketed vast sums on contract.
She plotted her next moves.
She paid us in gold to carry out certain procedures.
She booked us first-light passages on transport planes.
She sent word to Bartholomew.
We agreed never to speak.
Just this one time.
What we saw in the compound.

To not speak of convulsions, nor of vomiting.
To not speak of walling, that impact on muscle.
To not speak of standing, shackled,
rectal rehydration.
Ice-water baths harsher than presented.
To scream, drag, cut, hooded, dragged,
slapped and punched.
Taped—partially nude—
and chained to a concrete floor.

Testimony of the Incarcerated as Secured
by R & G Enterprises

Outside the walls of the compound
squatting over debris, gutter children to sing,
accented English, perfectly executed.
Once we knew of a rogue portal, the game,
eternal climate change, checkmate.
     Whoso will sit in the court of Al-Rashid.
Once we knew of children, branded for sale,
     *Ransomed, Healed, Restored, Forgiven,*
     markings to appear on entire brigades,
their arms, their biceps turned.

*This regime, clamped, electric,*
poured hot,
water to find cotton,
dried first, burnt,
thirty of us, our cell 2.5 × 2.

Rubber sticks and acid
to shut sense from screaming, a timbre
inside, never to see the blue sky.
Outside, thousands marching.
We, who once controlled, ordered, clicked and procured.
Now waifs, inducers of dreams
———gesturing and slow.

Later, we spoke of the Time of Before.
Seated, we made ourselves sing "The Fall of Baghdad."

Everything that was bad, was worse.
After five p.m., no one said the word *safe.*
Outside, textile workers, freed from free trade zones,
shouted exaltations: *Sherronda! Her flashing eyes! Her snake-coiled hair!*

## PRISONER TRANSCRIPTS, COLLATED AND KEPT
## BY R & G ENTERPRISES

### As Inscribed by T-LOHK: Transcript #1

We met the photographer known as — And —
We met the journalist known as — And then —
No, were never able to track them.
Some claimed two shots to the back of the head.

Several days later, off camera, those Guards,
Rajancrantz & Gabbarbhai:

*Look, you'll be dead soon, just sign here.*
*You're dreaming if you think she'll release you.*
*She'll make you fight.*

### As Secretly Recorded by T-LOHK: Transcript #2

The necessary injections.
The necessary tax evasions.
Mobile and acquired, that device.
The basement held the heat,
      many-roomed.

No mention of the detainees, erased.
Consortium would pay, and mercantile
bars of gold, alignment, the war to end —

Every revolution still needs a king.
No matter what father and son believed.

Overheard, Sherronda, before battle:
*Guards, bring me Rajancrantz and Gabbarbhai.*
*Make sure they bring the Panavision 8.*

**As Recorded: Transcript #3**

Pacifica to Mexico, Toronto to Paris,
Ahmedabad to Baghdad,
farmers indentured, farmers despairing.
Consortium produced story booklets:
landed families working the land, a rosy glow,
arid and hospitable, climate predictable,
the years a generation, into the number—
Chickens in their cages penned, a thousand tubers tilled.
No drought, no floods, no plague.
Fat hens and creameries. Market economies sustained.

**As Recorded: Transcript #4**

Imprisoned deep within the Green Zone,
a group of Seed Savers, once Consortium scientists:

She, a nurse bee, restrained
less than sixteen hours,
odour-introduced
fatty acid esters
proved inactive.
This contamination.
Cues rested, waiting
to be observed.
Sherronda, *our muse,*

called the bus-riding brigade.
Once we spent hours
investigative, island apiary.
Pushed open the sides,
brood cells, small wooden probes
then removed larvae with forceps,
using great care
not to puncture.

Then all the bees died.

We shared with resisters
all our learning, our cells
unlocked, we shuffled through.
*Jamais n'abolira le hasard,*
we learned to play jester, jump the fence,
no longer with the heart-belief
to say the word, *rain*, murmuring
instead about *fire*, weeping
smoke, to keep away Procne, weeping,
        we sang of tongues and men.

To Baghdad then we came, night,
into workhouse bunkers, our long incarceration
though we called out such names
only to obliterate, and joined
inside story, we sang of encounters
rendered, hidden in chanted codes;
vast transport planes, enormous containers,
Mexico–Paris–Ahmedabad–Baghdad,
fantastical travels, outside Perimeter, magenta sky,
freed maquiladora, textile workers
joined with Guild Makers, their voices
gathered deeper, *Sherronda! Sherronda!*

Inside the compound, we laughed,
the sound not anything——
Outside workers marched, chanting:
> *Her flashing eyes, her snake-coiled hair!*
> *First she freed us, now she'll feed us*
> *Marching rose on rose, fire on the gold*
> *Nary a needle nor a thread to knot*
> *Jumped the Fence! No more rain!*

### *Anthem of the Magnolia Brigade as Scripted by R & G Enterprises*

*Aromatic,* we the ragpickers of garbage mountains.
Unchained, we are returning to lamplight.
We, brown woman workers of Consortium.
Rags have voice, shuffling is voice,
discarded chairs, turned over,
the compound empty,
that is a voice.

Sing to the core,
heart inviolate.

We, being brought here.
We, inside the compound.
We, ragpickers from the Ghazipur landfills.
> Megacity salvagers, harvesting
> metal scraps, methane by the hour, spewed.
> Tuberculosis, sneaking seventy
> acres and fifteen storeys high, man-made
> earth movers, trommel machines, sticky mud,

dirty mattresses, suitcases and shoes—
from all this she saved us, transported us
monsoon to desert, filth hills to compound.

Renamed us as she renamed herself.
*Shanti-Ben to Sherronda,* Warrior Queen.
Our brown skin washed in the Sabarmati
brought to dust, to touch words, her findings, sweet,
whose name once was Shanti-Ben we recant,
commanded to recast, our past as well,
city to city, whole populations
unfolding foreigner memory,
methane and carbon dioxide,
this is what happened to us—
*Sherronda, our Sherronda.*
Once she was Shanti-Ben,
now her rule will know no end.

## SHERRONDA STEALS A LETTER

*Dear Future Survivors:*

We heard the laments of Beggars and Swords,
the same but not the same, they laughed and coughed.
We searched everywhere for the Lost Seasons.
Everyone we met spoke of the weather.
We found tattered parchments, an old oak box.
One letter, a scrap of handwriting, curled:

> Your hand crushing mine, our lips never kissed.
> Battle-weary in the Wet and the Dry—
> Kingsway a lost corridor, that small girl,
> penchant for making things, keys, gold locks,
> not her hair, mind you, coal black, glossy skin,
> under a culvert dry as bone they found
> remnants of an old PC, hard drive bust,
> the girl kept saying about messages
> transported away, and sent to the Lab.

*Guards,* cried Sherronda, *bring me R & G.*
Smiling, they accepted her offering.
*We'll keep it secret, we'll keep it safe.*
*Oh, yes, and about those Guards of the Fifth—*
Deserters from Consortium's east troops,
ragged, barefoot, they flocked to Sherronda.

The Curiously Disappearing Document Found
    and Hidden by Sherronda

Secret recording by Rajancrantz & Gabbarbhai,
as found by Sherronda inside an old oak box.
The more she touched the words, the faster they bled to fade.
She put the parchment down,
        even dropped it back into four dark corners.
She'd pick the parchment up again,
        each time her fingers met an edge——

From the Medical Records of——in the Year
    of the Reign:

Barrios, camps, outside Perimeter: lineups, designated areas;
Tower Juniper, Tower Cedar, Tower Ambrosia.
In Tower Ambrosia, a young girl, her name forgotten,
no one calls her, she is never spoken to—
Small build, dexterous, black hair, eyes slanted at their corners.
She never laughs, head bent most times, building things.
She calls them Finds. Her teeth, bones, unexamined.
Afternoons the heat: dust, that acrid curtain, wind whips red,
she finds places inside culverts where no streams,
fingers fast into hoarded, stolen, saved:
her six-wheeled machine, scrapped aluminum,
prized at the site where once Safeway,
the Battle of Kingsway, a song—
Fireside, she calls her toy.
There is no one around curious enough to ask—

Unnamed, without words, a series of lines, her pauses, dot-dash...
Long miles away, farther down the coast, at Consortium Lab JPL,
the designers study data, fascinated, curious and excited. All their
codes.

## SHERRONDA TAKES BAGHDAD

Green Zone flown in with no language
armed with old-century weapons
bodies to hang from cranes
sweltering heat, although winter.

At the bombed-out embassy, Consortium allies, abandoned.
Quick, so quick we didn't realize what—
Switchblade drones, bought and sold, market traders
concrete rubble, brick, twisted steel, bodies
strewn or dug, stray dogs roamed, abandoned homes.

We paid for our keep , foot soldiers
always marching ahead, Sherronda the Great.

Outside, brigades of warriors, parched voiced,:
*Shanti-Ben, sister of peace,* yet marching
*Liberator of the oppressed,* sweet-tongued
words to persuade you to do anything.
Golden locket at her throat, Kali's sword.
*Let all evil die and the good endure!*

## LEAVING BAGHDAD, SHERRONDA WINS OVER
## A NEW FOLLOWER

When the Guards brought Raphael to her tent
they both laughed: *Not another one to feed.*
*Oh well,* said Sherronda, shaking her head.
*Come with me boy, you can help carry seeds.*

—Raphael didn't say a word—just looked
at Sherronda, her warm hands, her unlined skin.
She taught him how to survive threshold wars:
the way all doors and gates stored their secrets,
the way calendars contained codes,
the way dawn and dusk, circles and lines
        might lead to a thousand steps.

Those first months after the Seed Savers' Rebellion
*SSR, SSR, See Where We Are.*
*This is how we sneak in, this is how we get in.*
*Baghdad to Paris, fare forward, east to west.*
*Ah, Sherronda, our Sherronda, can't look away!*
*Jamais, jamais, roll the dice, Jump the Fence.*
The whole while R & G filming, and yet
Sherronda and Raphael pretended,
        no watchers, not on them,
as if they could remain undocumented.
Months later, Raphael learned of a deal
        negotiated by R & G Inc.,
whose sole shareholder, Sherronda, purchased
        with the gold paid to her by the Tribunal—
        bond-secured, 5,465 satellites,
        orbital, digital, fast-tracked intel.

*I did it all for the good,* she kissed him.

Raphael smiled, her almond eyes, her gorgeous hair.

Late at night he'd sit, tent-side, Wi-Fi on,

armed with a new online moniker, tapping—

## *Return to Paris, and Victory… Almost*

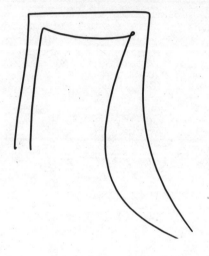

REMNANT: FOUND AT 2 SQUARE ADANSON, 75005, PARIS

*Seed Savers to the Makers' Guild*

Four rows of purl stitches and each column
To follow this pattern, to use black and white
White being the background colour
Black being the master colour

Due to the different heights of the stitches
On the wrong side of the rows
A stitch is flat, while a stitch is raised
Therefore, one can change which colour

So the basic idea is to create
In the colours one wants
When looking straight
But from an angle

There are no constraints
On the position of the purl/knit
A nearly infinite variety
Since one row may overshadow

Said Bartholomew: *Memorize this code*
Said Raphael: *Train me to decipher*
Said Sherronda: *Resistance without deeds—*
        *futile, by any means necessary*
When Bartholomew heard these words, he sighed.

## SHERRONDA MAKES IT POSSIBLE

Off Rue Monge at Rue Censure, Daubenton metro
  Quartier Jardin des Plantes
  Beggars & Swords, swept, fought
    singing, *Un coup de dés; jamais—*

Six women seated at a table quilt.
Their tongues clicking, soft voices whispering
*Green-eyed monsters, third-eye babies, neon blossoms...*

Two men meeting, one young, the other old:
red hair, grey eyes, a lilt to their speech——
A skein of terrible things: shortages,
shots sounded, barricades.

Everyone speaks of Sherronda's great skill:
*Bitcoin trader she gave us Big E blasts*
enough to store food, light cold homes past dark
semiconductors, huge stockpiles to last.

*Stitch, pull, stretch, framed: the shadow of a bee.*
Six women seated at a table laugh.

*Oh, you want to know about Sherronda?*
Last seen at the corner of Rue—Green Zone
*Who would have ever thought they'd bring it here?*
*City of light? City of dust, more like!*

Darkness settled on warriors and migrants.
Letters exchanged, glass jars counted, those seeds——
All the while the women with their slant smiles.
Later they said, *Well, we did like them looks.*

# IN THE HOUSE OF THE CATALYTICS

Exhaust emission controls, contraband,
Consortium unable to keep up with demand,
internal combustion, redox reactions.

Merry Band of Supply-Side Scavengers,
Sherronda, they cried, *we got three-ways, cheap!*
We got electrical generators,
      forklifts, trucks, buses,
            locomotives and ship parts,
all the nickel you'll need, plus sulphur free.
*Platinum, palladium, rhodium,*
lustrous silvery-white electronics.
Before-Time standard of living ensured.

This is what Sherronda promised her crew.
Scrap-dealer Guild won over by her wins.
*Nothing succeeds like victory,* she'd laugh.
Buyers and sellers, mercenaries too,
signed on to her brigades, fighting for cash.

*Nothing succeeds like action,* she'd whisper.
Raphael would kiss her breasts and forget,
scenes of his lover in battle, warrior
      wielding an axe, or worse,
          pressing buttons, intercontinental
          first-strike cruise missiles, Consortium fell.

All the while, R & G Enterprises searched
farmhouses, quarries, decrepit condos,
tumbled-down gymnasia, bankers' vaults.
*If by chance you see an oak box,* they said.

Bribes distributed: Big E ration cards,
water tokens from the privatized trucks,
mothers fought over those, desperate for drops.

# BATTLE CRY OF THE GOOD

*Sherronda's Victories as Recorded by R & G Enterprises*
*Small notebook left in a table drawer, 2 Square Adanson.*

Baghdad, Green Zone: winter, sweltering hot. Consortium unable
   to pay suppliers.
      Rumours of an oak box in an abandoned, bombed-out palace.
Ahmedabad: spring unusually wet, crops rotting. *Paramparik karigars*
   speak of seeing Bramah.
Paris: August, just the worst time of the year, humidex at 94, then hailstones.
      A brisk import market in Linden-Banyan hybrids, unthinkable
      then, flourishing trade now. Transport planes commandeered
      to search the Hidden Valley. Fly past for migrants. Sightings of
      Bramah. As if.

Everyone everywhere talking about that old oak box, no signs yet of any
   chalice pieces.
We remain, on assignment.

Signed,

Rajancrantz & Gabbarbhai

## SHERRONDA AT ODDS WITH SEED SAVERS

And repeated, about invasion, *tamarisk.*
Consortium approved, adapted to saline
    alkaline soils, light green foliage
    airy clusters, pink flowers
    hundreds of thousands
    then spreading by wind, over water
    into riparian, and deep rooted.
    It were deliberate, during the drought.
And so in this and many ways depleted.
All the streets disappeared under mud, dust
shadow people, heads bent, each step measured
names of cities from the past repeated
dirge chanting which made Sherronda cry out,
*Never mind, Aleppo, Grozny, never*
*forget what stakes, here, to win, forget seeds,*
hoarse with rage, her throat raw. Raphael looked
once, then turned away, hands on her hair, pushed
aside, she would not, could not, bear his touch
save at night, alone, the two of them safe
    at least for a little while.
Outside, approved arrondissements, seeds
smuggled imports, found countless ways, jars, sleeves.
Although banned, we gathered smoke bush
careful not to touch the stems.
Also—Rocky Mountain juniper, Preston lilac—
invasive brought Pacifica–Paris
illicit fragrance, pink, white, purple blooms
stored in Consortium hothouses, sold
by hired mercenaries to roving gangs.

Once, when still the Wet: ninebark
    finger to layers, vertical
    rounded and held
north, colder, birchleaf spirea
    deep green and oval—
We never knew, from one day to the next
waiting for signs, Portal messages, texts
sent clandestine or pulsed intermittent.

## SHERRONDA WINS PARIS FOR BARTHOLOMEW

Sweltering heat, torrential rains, trees stunted.
Inside the city walls, five clinics bombed.
Long after arrondissement destruction
Perimeter a hazing ground, Baghdad
letters sent, couriers waylaid, codes resent
tapped and broken, remaindered, supplies sold
inflated prices, supply chain woes, ground
troops fighting one another, no time to—
write it all down, take stock, repair, no time
amid chaos, Sherronda loved the cover
mayhem provided, relentless precision.
Consortium unable to provide
*the bare necessities*, Sherronda's Guards
sang and whistled as they chain-ganged farmers
food and soil, harvest and bread, new portions—
Sherronda emerging victorious.

*Look,* she cried one late afternoon
arms stained with blood, cigarette in one hand,
*I've brought us victory, now you go rule them.*
Later that day, she sent two secret letters
court couriers feared and disliked by all.
Their mission known only to Sherronda.
*Rajancrantz & Gabbarbhai, stay by me.*
Bartholomew pretended not to hear.
His heart sank, his mind too busy to care.
Housing and water, his burdens to bear.

Sherronda smiled and hired architects.
She planned a new HQ, fit for *The Good*—
iron and stone, steel frame, nine floors of brick.
Six wings connected, curving and central.
She hid the work orders for the slave labourers.
She commanded bronze and copper friezes
embossed and emblazoned with a giant *S.*

*Attention!* cried the street children, scattering
rags soaked, *Molotov!* Rocks, twigs, *IED Baby!*
One slingshot—abandoned in the mud.

Rajancrantz & Gabbarbhai, on assignment again,
time travel to retrieve plans from the past.
*These might work for us*, they told Sherronda.
She agreed.

### Drogheda

September Portal, 1649:
Depositions accumulated
beggars, widows and orphans, transported
adventured money transferred to the land.
Settlement, a plan to be repeated
data to the maps, landscape for the Act.
Degrees of guilt establishing forfeit:
*This is how it's done so pay attention*—
ratios a system, one fifth, three quarters
the province of Connacht and County Clare
deadlines given for transplanting or death
clearance a sweeping, strong-armed hand, embalmed.
Perimeter, a ten-mile stretch, reserved.
Certificates, categories, acres.
Meticulous and well-organized lines:
who to bring in, set down on farms, in homes
who to cast out, banished and broken harps.
Old tunes echoing down decades and danced
disinherited, in chains, still passed down
landless and remaining, to hew and to draw
carvers and weavers, crofters and potters
always a tinker, singing her sly songs
always following the line of the land.
Portal to Portal, we saw possibilities.

Pacifica to South Africa, a grid
plantation, reservation, blueprints
for the unwieldly and unlikely.
Maps and scrolls, charts and diagrams
Upon our return Sherronda exclaimed,
*All power lies in the design of things!*
>>>>>>

**Paris in an Earlier Time**

April Portal, 1789:
Hunger riots and pillaging of corn
Bray-sur-Seine, Rambouillet, Pont-Sainte-Maxence.
Pamphlets hand to hand: ten, twenty each day.
*Qu'est-ce que le tiers? Les droits des états—*
Tavern to suburb, outskirts of the poor
forerunners of July sang "Réveillon."
*Paper,* the workers said, skillful hands stained.
*Black bread and lentils, no wheat for our tongues.*
Sentence and execution, effigies
carried to the Place Royale, night, the streets
resounding; ragged dawn, attacked
plundered, the people, stones to guns, the troops
barged barricades, suburban mobs breaking
open doors, at Villejuif and the Bicêtre Prison.
No accident, no brigands, or agents.
April, the People, forerunning July.
Margins shape-shifting into the centre.
*I'm all for history,* Sherronda laughed.

>>>>>>

### Europe

Winter Portal, short-lived and fiery, 1848:
Barley, wheat, potatoes, staple crops failed.
Fatigue in the soil drove mass migrations.
Lower wages, higher prices, brewed fear.
Credit inflation made the land fallow.
Clearances and commodities, railways and sheep, steel.
Bonds, shares to raise capital, savings and loans.
Monarchs against barricades, bullets to books.
Came February and Manifesto
street to tavern, basement printing presses
history, a dialectic—freed, enslaved
one surviving page, first draft, handwritten.
Vienna, Berlin, Paris and Milan.
Artisans against proletarians
*Sowing seeds*, they sang, barricades to trains
discontent and masses, liberty taxed.
*Upheaval*, our cycle, *years to the Wars*.
We made a note to warn Sherronda.

### Ahmedabad

Monsoon Portal, 1848, echoing:
Overheard, transmitted interception—
one thousand, two hundred artisans and labourers
white marble edifice, a Jain temple—
come the famine, and many would shelter.
Hutheesing legacy, *aabas*-style draped
*pathola* saris, nine yards of cut silk
tiny needles, lehenga embroideries.

Textured panels East-West mixture
the age, the years, outside revolt—
inside, luxury, chamber to gilt beds.
The Moon, her many mistresses, singing:
*Scheherazade*, one thousand tales within——
We knew Sherronda would approve.
Perimeter, that Detention Centre:
just outside, Beggars and Swords sang, roving,
*Come ye in, airborne, after, masks and hoods,*
*masks and hoods.*
Ahmedabad to Baghdad, we would arrive
but first——
>>>>>>

### *Moscow*

Early Spring Portal, 1917, unhinged:
city-wide strikes, Nevsky Prospekt rumbled.
Stupidity or reason? Whips, guns, bayonets.
Women in line for hours, bitter cold
three, four, five, ten percent inflation sparked
food shortages, arrests and then almost
unnoticed, March, thousands from the bread lines
red flags with banners, Cossacks to disperse,
*Some disorders, nothing too serious.*
We heard, stopped to raise our heads, repeated,
*Some disorders, nothing too serious.*
When we repeated these words to Sherronda
she laughed again and rolled up documents,
*I can't wait to see Bartholomew's face.*

All our plans assembled, we gripped iron
door handles sharp fixed to committee rooms
where sat Bartholomew in chambers, writing
orders to redistribute wealth and lands.
Our silk jackets emblazoned with red thread.
Entourage for Sherronda who strode ahead.
*Paris, we arrive again, souviens!*
Crowds gathered outside Perimeter singing,
> *Un coup de dés*
> *jamais, jamais.*
> *Jumped the Fence*
> *you should, too.*

Bartholomew's Guards refused us entry.

# The Short Rule of Bartholomew the Good

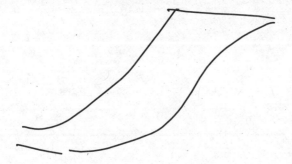

>>>>>>

## ENDLESS DAYS OF DRY

Roaming deserted streets, girls sang letters
*Spin, rotate, tilting and orbital, Our Sun—*

Lawn painters, they sprayed each blade of grass, green.
Subsoil dried, incapable of moisture.

First the heat, then everything burnt down.
Under the viaduct we'll crown him king.

*B* is for Bartholomew, supply chains
restored enough to feed us, Big E on—

We're all soon to become beggars and moan
*Farewell Summer, unlike anything known,*

*you've left us bare, broken, reduced to ash.*
*Come, Bramah, find us, make everything right—*

And then after months of dry, the deluge.
Seeds stored in our pockets, husk to sieve, wrapped.

# CONSORTIUM DEGRADED, THE RESISTANCE UPHELD

By water, patched-up pipelines, privatized:
Perimeter ration cards, a brisk trade—
Bartholomew's Edict on Equity
at first strictly enforced, then, the gaming—

By fire, land allotments for farmers
seasonal coupons handed out for cattle
incentives paid in kind for crews to dig
at first, harvests yielding enough and then—

By earth, city condo blocks reassigned,
villas and mansions carved up for the poor.
No child to sleep on the street they all agreed,
midnight curfews obeyed at first, and then—

By wind, airport transport, shipping lanes, freed.
Matchsticks to mobiles, wireless signals
energy spun, propeller arms rigged high
city lights and hydro dams, cubic weights.

> *Nothing like Before*, at least sort of normal
> At first everyone willing to make do——

Outside Perimeter, the boys chanted:
*Right as rain, good as new.*

*Jumped the Fence, you should too—*
> *Jumped the Fence, you should too—*

Until the first meeting of the Commune
Bartholomew kept the oak box hidden
raised skyward on a plinth made by the Six
Carpenters of Baghdad, indentured, freed
after the first fall of Consortium
inside the box, pieces of the chalice.
What once belonged to Dr. Anderson.
*Pieces of the lost,* we would whisper.
Committee members deputized to rule.
Water lines fixed, freshwater dams restored:
grocery store workers formed a Night Shift.
*Bread and Roses,* sang the morning sweepers.
Makeshift schools assembled in parking lots.
Scrubbed, shining faces—for this we had fought.

## AS FOUND ON BARTHOLOMEW'S DESK

*Locator: situé Square Adanson, 75005*
*Signifier: in the year of the reign 20XX*

Where Bartholomew, and handed, his papers
and would pace parquet, the window
dormer offering, that edifice
a series of roses, terracotta. Held.

His fragments, a site of research
inside language, emanations, echo
what he had found in the razing
saved animals, species hybrid.

On the desk, inside
lists of the sacred, commonly known
maps for reconstruction, dams and highways
plans for solar power generators.

An archive, and there to spend
hours, the afternoon, and waiting—
expended, those breaths
memory, shards of—

Outside the barricades the hungry sang,
*We won't mind makeshift,*
>*we patched over all our things*
>*we'll make do with the New Normal*
>*just make sure we have*
>*enough to eat.*

## BARTHOLOMEW TRIES HIS BEST

*Climate change disrupted Consortium—*
that's what everyone said at the railways;
from the Dry to the hunger and then we—
Seed Savers, resisters to join forces.
Deserters from the Guards to Sherronda
her battalions always at the ready
to raise Bartholomew, to call him *Good.*
He never wished for crown or gun and yet
shortages forced him to centralize rule
*disorder, disaster, drought and famine*
each of these words muttered under his breath
urging him to numbers, charts, documents
how to make things work, *how to restore calm*
he told himself, breath warming chilled fingers
past midnight, candles flickering—Data:
supply line allocations, Big E on
bombed wind farms resuscitated, alarms
sounding at all hours, never enough
to feed the hungry, to shore up the banks.
Deserters from Consortium, armed Guards
eager to join Sherronda's troops, aground.

By Order of Sherronda the Great: camera numbers defaced.


Locator: Paris, Fifth Arrondissement, Perimeter
barricades maintained
In the Year of the Reign 2106
Monitor Status: Unexplained power shortage disrupted
transmission.

Partial Recording, retrieved at a later date by R & G Enterprises
Minutes of Secret Tribunal Meetings
Said Sherronda, *You'll have to count on me.*
Silence around the Tribunal chamber.
Outside doors guarded by Rajancrantz & Gabbarbhai.
Said Sherronda at the meeting's tail end
    Quiet voice as she turned to her two Guards
    *No record of this meeting shall survive.*
And did Rajancrantz and Gabbarbhai agree?
Of course they did! Then exited to do her commands.

# BARTHOLOMEW FACES THE ODDS

Water merchants rehired: Big E, on—
reading after nightfall, a luxury
restored without having to light candles.
We sighed with heads bent to hear no more bombs.
Trembling hands, contraband cigarettes, smoke—
memory shards sunk, barbed wire and nailed boots
shoeless child soldiers, Fifth Guard deserters
textile workers all pledged to Sherronda.
First light she'd drill them, and we'd watch
later to record, *munay bo majah chay,* she'd say, laughing.
We'd seen her at the fall of Ahmedabad.
If not for us, who would then remember?

Lash, heel, duck, thrust, flung, caught, crawled and swinging.
Slithered, tangled, kicked, shuddered, and again, crawled.
Dusty streets churned to mud with blood, shrapnel
exploding shells, armaments from Before-Time centuries.
Sprawled, thrown, grabbed, rolled, shipped. Torn, slipped, dragged, lurching
survivors, prisoners granted amnesty
by order of Bartholomew, although
scorned by Sherronda who scoffed. *No mercy
rare as hen's teeth,* she'd scowl. He disagreed.
*We'll need them in the coming days, we will——
We must rebuild,* Bartholomew would urge.
*Anything cracked, hammered, dropped, we must fix.
Help me return to a New Normal, please!*
No one said anything, just kept walking.

### Consortium Cuts Its Losses, Regroups

Remnants of Consortium slunk away.
Executive Princes, controlling shares.
Deep supply chain connections to farms, food.
Tangibles enough to recruit back Guards.
Mergers negotiated, acquisitions——
They knew Bartholomew would need product
distribution lines and technical skills.
He knew this, too, late at night surrounded
maps, messages, a thousand requests, threats
everyone wanting everything restored.

# BARTHOLOMEW'S SUPPLY CHAIN DISASTERS

Shortages, goods waylaid, stalled and buried
shipping containers rusting in rail yards
masks, vaccine vials, semiconductors
plastic polymers, bicycles and toys.
Free trade zones: trucks, ships, planes, cranes and forklifts.
No oil, and coal caverns depleted.
Backlot backlogs, no raw materials.
Freight scarce, what once were cheap, plentiful
annual contracts tossed, the end of non-stop.
24/7, Beggars and Swords jeered
point-to-point transfer, dream-time luxuries.
For a while we waited for rates to drop.
Wildfires burnt up our rail yards out west.
Hands shook, we knew we'd not survive this test.

Pacifica ports filled with stranded ships.
Weeks turned to months, containers as shelters.
Routes and capacity, families on hire.
Bartholomew did his best, we couldn't——

We took to living portside, rummaging
warehouses, dockside and rusted, rats run
their red eyes gleaming at sunset, scurrying——

Snow drought or sirocco-sifted wounds, hearts
bodies found in debris, after the bombs.
We noted a thousand fatal errors.
We attempted transmittal to the front.
We implored Guards to tell Bartholomew.
We took for granted: products on store shelves
       to-do lists fulfilled, just walk up the hill.

Our children roamed in rags singing softly,
*Who will come for us, remember our names?*
*We had everything, now we have nothing*—

# FOLLOWERS OF BARTHOLOMEW

Nights without electricity, endured.
Rhythms will have to change, we told ourselves.
First, we needed to figure out, freezing
penicillin, drugs, vaccines, all our lists.
Cities reimagined, top to bottom.
We refused to indulge in nostalgia.
Consortium luxury, a memory.

We remembered what the Oracle warned:
as recited by Bramah to Bartholomew
      *Consortium will shift*
      *collective to oligarch*
      *ask yourself or you will become*
      *strongman rising, long shadows*
      *history a curse, wars' motivator*
      *grain disruptions, hunger a stalking horse*
      *supply chains wrecked, you'll be blamed*
      *migrations, displacement*
      *disasters await*—We remembered
Bartholomew coughing, head bent
all his many tasks and burdens
how to rule in catastrophic times.
His silence, his shoulders slumped—
Years later others would speak
versions of these truths
Bartholomew told us that Bramah said
*Be careful.* We knew he tried his best.

♛

## FOLLOWERS OF SHERRONDA

We who would walk Perimeter, those crows
a chorus, under feathers fluffed. Outside
batteries and armaments, we hoarded.
We saw her mastiff hounds running at night.
She named them Hardy, Havelock and Hotspur.
We heard their war cries, breaking the pale dawn.
All she wanted was to win.

## WORSENING CONDITIONS, AGAIN

All the things that Bartholomew couldn't stop.
Consortium agents with enough funds.
Rumour was that Bramah helped them,
secret treasury funds, world bank vaults, unlocked,
words Bartholomew refused to repeat.
Each morning at dawn he'd send messages
data retrieval to measure water,
        port blockages, supply chain shortages.
All the things over which he had no rule.
Although they paid him lip service, he knew
Tribunal executive had their ways,
satellites secured, enough oil and gas.
Big E and Wi-Fi ration tickets sold.
Enough to placate anonymous mobs
busy roaming, restless, click, tap and scroll.
All the things he couldn't know, he kept on.
Nights when in the next room, Raphael sat,
        click, tap, swipe,
neither of them would mention all the comments,
        bots and numbered aliases
                taglines replete:
a thousand a day followed Sherronda,
        likes and replies, hearts and winking faces,
                underscore and lower-cased.

♛

## Sounds Echoing Across Perimeter

Small, ragged street children always chanting:

> And then to Haddon Hall, sing Patch 'n Mend
> Start before sunrise that long glowing light
> Oh, once we could, and used to be growing—
> lettuce and chard, parsley and basil, green
> leaves to pluck in the late afternoon warmed
> testing for ripeness, those smooth silver spoons
> Come tap melons, pinch sweet kernels of corn
> plumpness and thickness, pull, break the bright light
> Oh forever and a day, once we could—
> alas, alas, the Hidden Valley gone.

Outside the Fifth Arrondissement, a grove
five plane trees and an oak, branches spreading
six-sided enclave, filled with fennel, sage
purple stalks, echinacea dripping
beeswax and laurel leaves, acorns and twigs.
*Whither the seeds of the wild dandelion?*
Beggars and children chain-ganged to harvest.
Barbed wire enclosures, armed Guards on watch.
Green and golden for those who could afford
bribes to the Guards, who claimed to protect us
their voices rough, fading——
*Jumped the Fence, and You Should, Too.*

# BARTHOLOMEW BATTLES THE SEASONS

The end of temperate, wind, rain, flooding—the end of benign;
  unpredictable
savage catastrophic: volumes of water—in denial, we refused to believe.
Earth saying, *Get Out*, we couldn't relax, we let go plans for comfort,
  luxury—
We learned the hard way, *normal* gone for us. First the drains
overflowed, sewage pumps stopped. Big E ration cards in high demand,
  then—

>   pounding heavy constant
>   buckets sheets drumming
>   rivulets sluicing waterfalls
>   splash to drip faster roaring
>   pools rising sodden ground
>   disappeared—low sky grey blanket
>   sheen to force-flow rushed
>   slurp, the mud; rise the flood!

*I never seen water like this*, he said; each hour dykes measured,
then overrun, patched burlap and never enough sand.
Swollen river leaping across divides. Evacuees without any homes.
Then the tanks rolled in, highways collapsing.

>   Night bleeding into day
>   bandaged by wind
>   unfurled: stretched stents
>   barely upholding dawn
>   sodden canvas tent
>   doors flapping open
>   candle flickering
>   an old oak box floating away—

♛

Bartholomew studied his patient maps
how to resuscitate his last battalions.
Foot soldiers, we waited, his coughing words,
shawl draped over shoulders bent not by age,
worn shifting fabric, once royal red, faded.
Foreheads creased, hands wringing, we awaited news.
Airports long abandoned for civilians.
Ships' passage the only way out.
Scared, for a while we pulled together, then——
We hired on to private Space Corp. X
tapped one of their apps, swiped up, then pressed send—
logistics personnel, nice house and car.

# *Civil War in the Wet*

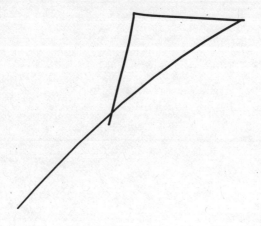

REMNANT BALLADS OF THE WET

## Heard Unseen, Those Last Aunties of the Wishing Well

wind and rain, until our cisterns rise full
burn the sun, until our skin won't blister
wind and rain, low grey clouds, breeding trouble
sagging ceilings, clogged drains, laboured breath
wind and rain, virus spores, dark days' return
arms and legs branded, ransomed children roam
wind and rain, Before-Times gone, this good rule
ends wind and rain, Bramah, will you come again
burn the sun for our return, green the land
wind and rain, rivers deep, we'll not yet sleep—

## Seen on the Streets Outside Perimeter, Pacifica's Edge

*Belly full of worry, full of the sads.*
*Crust of bread, a little drink, all the bads.*
Beggar with Swords, Swords with pens
joined forces with In-Betweens, *they and them*
banded together, their echoing songs.

## Found Pinned to an Oak Tree, Hidden Valley/Price Park

Grandmother cautioned us against protest:
*Time spent shouting, better served by making—*
tools to till, pots to cook, wool to weave clothes
no good ever came from men armed with guns
winter fuel carried in yellow plastic
jugs: crypto and rigged, children danced on straw
fathers linked arm to shoulder, their slogans—
*Flags and sticks, jugs and rigs,* sighed Grandmother.
Sherronda's face impassive, she paced nights.

Splinter group executives paid her well.
How to put chaos and unrest to use.
*Nobody wanted this war*, they said.
Grandmother saw though, streets flowing with red.

# EVENTS MULTIPLY

First it were the drought because of accelerated.
Then famine, because of drought, food wars grew.
Food wars and unrest, slouching to the Wet.
Structural erosion, famine to fall
Consortium unable to provide:
no longer capital, nor any shops.

Paper hoarded, lumber so scarce, a find.
Bartholomew repaired our supply lines.
Capital strikes, though, he could not control.
*Last night the two moons laughed through clouds of rain.*
No longer chained, cast-off children swept streets
singing of the time, New Normal or what——
We heard them speak of the Day of the Burnt Hand.

We didn't want, we tried not to, but then
starvation or the threat of it forced us:
obedience in exchange for heat, light.
We avoided posting our opinions.
We looked away and found ourselves fast-tracked:
access to better quality schools, food
rationed in larger proportions, stubs saved.
We didn't want to vote for them but did.
Sector after sector, returning books
banned if too critical of consumption.
Trade-offs to purchase, delivery times raised.
We looked away, those ragged couriers' shoes.
Came the day of the Reinstatement, we stay home.
Big E restored, all our cable channels.
*Nothing too extreme,* we were sure to say.
We ignored the pleas of migrant workers.
Came the day when we knew we were all safe.

Trains running on time and waterworks fixed.
*Sure, there was fighting,* bloody but distant.
We looked away when we heard their slogan:
*Choice is my liberty, my wealth my right.*
What could Consortium do but concede?
Big E commandeered for social media.
Followers with their lower case handles.
Electronic mobs, eager to tap, share.

*To Whom It May Concern*

**Battlefield of the Barricades**

House-to-house combat inside Perimeter
Bodies strewn, streetside, machine-gunned down
We crept among the dead to the wounded
maimed arms, legs, parched voices pleading, *Water.*

**Machine Gun Rhapsody**

Assault or sniper, shoulder aim and fire
AK-47, Heckler & Koch
C9s to load up seven hundred rounds
Lethal, old Portals no longer guarded
Once were the sweeter seasons, temperate rain
Hand-cranked, six-barrelled, central shaft released
Sherronda hired Portal Raider Gangs (PRGs)
pistol grips and triggers, skilled iron sights
Trained annular, shrouds around the front post
Three-dot, straight eights, gold beads, tritium glow
Stolen code entry, past wars' armaments
Fibre optics, ambient light falling
Air rifles and muzzle loaders, fast work—
Winter's Midnight, opening, there they would lurk
Calibre cruise missiles, strategic hits
Hostile takeovers, private space stations
Offshore migrant processing, increased by—
*Stop the Boats*, screamed the online newsfeeds
Detention centres built, worldwide networks
All these things accelerated chaos.
Loved by war profiteers, a handful of—

# UNDERGROUND FROM SAVAGE SKIES

Brigade workers inside Perimeter
scrambling, they pushed to underground stations
endless piercing, a shriek inside to out:
*Where will we go?* Alone labouring here
no one knew who'd called in the air attacks:
*No way Sherronda would do this to us—*
whispers and moans, steps hurried or measured
red suitcases clattering down subway stairs
earth layers, vaulted steel and concrete
built back by Bartholomew now crumbling
Wi-Fi limited access, phones tossed down
voices rising deep inside the ground, layers—
Outside, above, homes collapsed, matchstick frail.
Consortium missiles, air raid sirens
wailed in the morning and no birds sang.
*Ghosts roam stolen land, Time brings affliction.*
*Who will come for us?* the children cried out.
And again, the air whistled, lethal wails
raining down dust, betrayal and despair.

Outside Swords sighed, derisive, in chains:

*IED, baby, IED*
*Your bombs, our arms, boom!*
*Hypersonic, new world tonic*
*Our bombs, our arms, boom!*
*Save your threads, baby*
*Doom-Time's coming soon.*

These chants echoed in the blue-grey of dusk
sword tips clinking on iron, transported
convoys ever forward, the eastern front.
*Recent sharp increases in oil prices.*
This the Swords repeated more than once.
When they came to the place of the four winds
scrawled jagged inside a bombed city hall
pandemic deaths at home unrecorded
people born, dying undocumented.

## PINNED TO CY-BOARD #9

*Dear Future Survivors,*

Weather a portal, how we tore ourselves
*Partition or borders, what are we for?*
Nights in encampment barefoot in the mud
we couldn't stop sea surfaces rising.
Ice Age forgotten, now caught, drought to flood.
Consortium funded data, disproved.
Private trips to space promised solutions.
Whose side to believe in, we couldn't choose.
Spirit emanations, fragments of life
warmed, tossed, spun, virulent shaking, unstopped.
Each whirling, battering vortex scattered
photos, letters, notes, diaries, archives, lost.
Expectations and longings from the past
the last summer, the perfect spring, all gone.

*May, April, October*
words said like beads
to rub memory
> *When the rain sang to us in the night*
> cried Beggars and Swords.
> *Jamais, Jamais.*
*May, April, October*
months of the unlucky
Bartholomew and Sherronda battled.
We just wanted a return to normal.
We just wanted to count again on the Seasons.
Night of the Burnt Hand, that was October.
Hundreds lost their lives, fighting for what—
a crust of bread, a lean-to shed, Big E passes.
Winter ground us with snow drought and ice storms.

Night of the Great Taking, that was April
　　*If your countenance sweet and your heart, kind—*
　　　　or so legend said.
Night of Defeat, when bodies stacked up, ferocious losses.
Consortium found ways to funnel money.
Sherronda kept winning, battle to bridge.
Bartholomew's troops pushed back, step by step.

# GETTING BY, NOT CHOOSING SIDES BECAME HARDER

A great many said nothing, saw nothing.
Knew nothing except lying low, quiet,
workers hired to farm, dug ditches too,
looked away when the first trucks arrived.

Raised chickens, harvested eggs, no eye contact,
market days hushed after air raid sirens
stopped, no ceasefire, just occupation.
Days counted, step by step, from bed to field,

past curfew, not a sound save troops marching,
front lines extended, far away enough——
pretence necessary inside, heads down
factory time clocks punched,

unobtrusive, they knew to stay grey, still
sameness night after night a virtue held
in whispers they knew not to make a fuss,
not to call attention, seeing little
saying little, if at all, the People.

*

Piles of rubble, glass, and twisted metal,
our homes slipping under the rising seas.

# THE PLOT AGAINST BARTHOLOMEW

Dubious escalation of sanctions.
He was forced to sign supply-side oil deals.
Consortium the winner in the end;
not an ending at all, mere beginning.
Again Perimeter and free trade zones.
Capitalism reinventing the stakes.
Shanti-Ben to Sherronda knew to play
odds were and against and took risks, marched on.
Readiness that year, a set of actions
bandages rolled, masks sewn, home fires burning.
Oil, gas, coal, wind, solar, spitting atoms
we'd hired on for them all, astonished
      when nothing worked
      and then, the fall——R & G Enterprises.
Busy, busy, Big E, wireless
      mobs for hire, anonymous accounts
thousands followed, then millions
      Sherronda's posts, *lmk how I'm doing*
bots to Bitcoin, posted back, rapt likes
      click, tap—on the streets of Paris
outside Perimeter in Pacifica
satellites fired up, ready for use
      beamed to locations, coordinates set to rain.
Baghdad in fifty-degree heat, winds roared.
Scorched afternoons where Green Zone battles raged:

Swords and Beggars               fought Magnolia Brigades

rivulets of blood ⬡ mixed with dust
              chants raised,
       *Good as new,*
          *right as rain,*
       *Jumped the Fence,*
          *you should, too.*
Consortium Tribunals bided their time.

## TO WHOM IT MAY CONCERN

Unverified Cy-Board Post, Attributed to T-LOHK,
Itinerant Scribe.
Found and Then Hidden by Rajancrantz & Gabbarbhai

### *Bartholomew's Last Stand*

We crossed out of Perimeter, borders,
hedges, train tracks, a long line of fir trees.
Long after the wars, food supply chains, scarce.

His trial impending or so they say.

Befriended, this small girl brings him androids.
At night she squats roadside, chanting her words.
Rumour has it she is named Sonali and is Sherronda's child.

We can only decipher a few here:

> *Right as rain*
> *good as new*
> *Jumped the Fence*
> *you should too.*

Her poor left arm branded with hexagons.

Some say all of Bartholomew's followers
abandoned him, even his own son.
Two miscreants follow us every step.
Their black silk jackets stained.
Cameras filming all the time.

## SHERRONDA PERSUADES RAPHAEL

Said Raphael, before:

*Everything stored up inside my body*
*Oh I am Fortune's Fool and cannot, yet—*

Said Sherronda, after:

*Silence descends upon my iron heart*
*No touch ever warm enough to melt me.*

## RAPHAEL'S CHOICE AS DOCUMENTED BY RAJANCRANTZ & GABBARBHAI

Inside, Abigail's only son,
     child of that bittersweet union
     Bartholomew's boy and adored—
     Once were so happy to have found
          family to live by, and then,
          and now, inside with his thoughts
          careening back and forth
          If it were poison stolen from the Aunties
          if it were slow and incremental
          *Arsenic, tried and true,*
          he'd never say, he looked away
     remembering—

Outside, brigades of workers, now warriors:
*Shanti-Ben, sister of peace,* they marched on
liberators of the oppressed, sweet-tongued
firm in their belief they could persuade anyone to do anything:
*golden locket at her throat, Kali's sword.*
*Let all evil die and the good endure!*

Good thing we intercepted his vain attempts.
He tried to give it one last shot.
He tried to send word to his father.

>>>>>>

## Rajancrantz & Gabbarbhai Productions

We both wore matching silk bomber jackets.
Emblazoned in red script on our shoulders:
  The Play's the Thing.

No man, not even this Bartholomew
could resist our methods, so we pulled out
from a seam sewn into his filthy coat
this letter, it begins,

> Dear Raphael
> Found: in the year of the reign 2107

Inscribed in a blue notebook, blue ink:

> My great longing is to share the story about all of every-
> thing that's happened, to me, to this world, to time,
> space, tilted, set-off, another axis, so that the story will
> become—And webbed, a trap, a net, spell to cast on each
> plant, all the names, trees, the Secret River, the Good-
> Bye River, River of a Thousand Names, oh for days in our
> Hidden Valley, those nights, numinous, the story sent
> out, tucked, pocketed, the footsteps of migrants, Guards,
> the city, decayed, underground, uplifted to mountains,
> bony spine of a continent, ridged, wild winds, ocean cur-
> rents, broad and vast, long lines, fingering wool so strong,
> warm enough to reach and grab and hold, to capture,
> retain, stop Time, move, return.

### R & G Prop Department, Crew's Statement

This oak box hewn huge, needing a hundred men to lift
    weight of all the killings, inscribed documents.
This wood found west, outside Perimeter
    once as tall as cathedrals, those spires.

Our orders written pasted, inlaid bark
from every ancient tree tagged, found cut down
    catalpa and birch——we filmed it all. Panavision.
    Deluxe colour.
Then we hid the cannisters.
Outside Detention Centre C, beggars
    sweep and sing, their faint echoes rising up:

    *We ain't never going back*
       *'cause every star, a sun*
    Draco in three thousand
       *Vega in twelve*
       *Sherronda or Shanti-Ben*
       *Who knows when*
       *she'll rise again*
       *Jump the Fence!*

Assistant to Rajancrantz: "But what does it all mean?"
Assistant to Gabbarbhai: "Not sure—just use some of it."
Assistant to Rajancrantz: "We could write labels, boom, boom."
Assistant to Gabbarbhai: "We need to bury all our records."
Assistant to Rajancrantz: "How about something like this?"

Legend: Sherronda's body confiscated, kept hidden by her fanatic loyalists, followers of the Magnolia Brigade, they scattered unto the hills.

TESTIMONY OF THE MERCENARIES REASSEMBLED

After the fall of Bagdad in the year——
The dead:

an assignment, to count them—
    we were speaking then of three mortuaries

we were aware. An appalling stench.
    After about a month—

,we were noticed and saw with our own eyes.
    Bodies without heads.

We were looking over, and our eyes—
    on the street, outside Perimeter

head, without body.

We gave notification, his faith, unknown
    dog's head stitched on—
except this version rejected and claimed
    conversion to a belief only in history—

*dialectic*—we entered the courtyard of the ~~mosque~~—
    converted library to synagogue
        to temple to meth lab
mercantile, videos bought and sold

those executions. How might we describe.
Impossible.

We were cognizant of beards; although obscured—
and came to see those soldiers, stripped, hooded
        the courtyard, where traded, tapes to show how—
imprisoned, exectued, or exiled.

Two former Guards paid us well.
They wore these jackets, matching shiny black.
Emblazoned with red letters, threaded silk.
We didn't ask any questions.

## SHERRONDA'S TESTIMONY TO THE COMMITTEE
## FOR PUBLIC SAFETY

Songs of the high pastures—
      *by any means necessary*, I said.
Before the deep snows,
      I'd imagine vistas grazed over
flocks of sheep and goats, shepherds shot, deserters fled
        my army combat boots, at my back, a hundred thousand
          to march under night vision—shadows
past the suburbs, beggars calling, *Zayouna,*
      where alleyways—a stray shot, gunfire—
        metal on concrete ricocheting way past
those tree nurseries, *Zafranyia,* outside the City Gates.
In spring I'd plan another campaign, by now three hundred thousand
        all chanting my name,
      up the Tigris, river floods coming down.

♛ ♛ ♛
>>>>>>


I tell you all this, so you understand
      my sacrifice, humble soldier rising:
Baghdad centralized for our East armies.
      The heat punishing. No matter. I occupied.
*Let All Evil Die and the Good Endure,*
      my troops, raucous, demanding we spill blood.

# The Fall of Bartholomew the Good, 2107

# AUTUMN AT THE GATE OF FOREBODING

Once gentle and temperate, slow, sweet hours
now winds scoured thin soil, torrential rains
flash floods, particulate-laden, grey skies
*Seasons of mist,* sighed roaming beggar boys
scraps of meat, hunks of bread, gutters cleaned.
Ditch diggers for roads washed out, fallen huts
Perimeter's edge blurred; west-side roofs carved.
*Mellow fruitfulness,* cried Sword Girls, jabbing
mobs circling around grain warehouses.
With the coming of the Wet, coughs and colds.
Long lines under bridges to see medics.
Messages to Bartholomew waylaid.
Sherronda's Guards searched every letter sent.
Save one beggar boy, quick fingers, head bent——

### As Recorded by Rajancrantz & Gabbarbhai

We heard child labourers, chained, singing faint:
*IED baby, your bombs, our arms, boom!*
*IED baby, inside, outside, boom!*
*Freedom fighter, terrorist, who's right, wrong?*
*We just want enough to eat, been so long.*

We filmed the rain, atmospheric rivers:
pounding heavy constant
buckets sheets drumming
rivulets sluicing waterfalls
splash to drip faster roaring
pools rising sodden ground
disappeared—low sky grey blanket
sheen to force-flow rushed
slurp, the mud; rise the flood.

One lone fortune teller spoke of future battles.
No one with the time to pay attention.

## SHERRONDA BETRAYS BARTHOLOMEW

Inside, Bartholomew,
fingers weary, he'd signed false confessions.
He'd not once heard from his son.
Outside, walls of the compound, graffiti:
*Ghost Worker*
*Lives Here*

translated from the French to Arabic to English, unverified:
*Le travailleur*
*(L'ouvrier)*
*de fantôme*
*vit ici.*

Embedded notes in a black leather notebook.
  Botany interspersed with 3-D sketches
  a series of weapons—
    *five times faster than five miles per second.*
  Who would foretell, mass graves, bombed hospitals.
  Eyes downcast, the open market, rain, rare as hen's teeth.
  It were Rue Mouffetard, merchants.
  It were Abu Nuwas street, toward the Tigris.
  Found: a sheaf of papers. Published reports.
  Familles de Plantes, *in the environs of Paris.*
    Experiments, by means of,
    plants grown in small pots,
    Rue de Jardin du Roi, *herbarium specimens,*
    shells, animal remains, to compile and observe,
    lists, a catalogue, notes of which survive.
  There I was, had been, would again.
  Would take the lift, would stare out.
  Pantheon, a view of history.
  Not knowing until much later.

### *Inside Consortium's Hexagon-Shaped Courtroom*

Hundreds of spectators, heads bent to phones:
as promised and on time, new Wi-Fi, strong.
Crammed to the front doors, marble steps defaced,
armed gangs, hustlers hawked gallery tickets.
*Silence, silence all round,* roared the jurists.
Blood dripped slowly down his cheek, shackled gait.
We who had seen him crowned, stared in disbelief.

Outside, beggars chanted,
    *IED, baby,*
    *the good's all over,*
    *just you wait and see.*

*After the Verdict, mayhem in the streets.*
Swords, their cheeks tear-stained, chased by Guards, screamed loud:
*Let all evil die and the good endure!*
Inside their pockets, fragments of torn text,
a letter, untouched by Guards, too unsure
to search those quicksilver limbs, fast moving.
Outside the Detention Centre, armed men.
By night fall a ragtag bunch of beggars
hauled cans of stolen red paint, giant letters:
*Un coup de dés, jamais, jamais.*

*After the Sentencing, Orders: Signed & Sealed*
On the desk of Sherronda,
a set of gold rings, engraved, pressed red wax:
*Ransomed Healed Restored Forgiven.* RHRF.

Tossed into the hands of the Magnolia Brigade.
They muttered as they marched with the prisoner:
    *As if a knife, but then a gun only.*
    *As if a bomb, but then a line of tanks.*
    *As if missiles, rocket launchers and drones.*
      All good an illusion.

# THE DISAPPEARANCE OF BARTHOLOMEW

R & G Productions, Crew Notes

of which little is known, no texts survive, save the
following:

At zero hundred hours:
12:00 a.m. = 00:00: Transport prisoner, first floor
Eiffel Tower 58
zero hours, or start of day
12:30 a.m. = 00:30: Ensure Tribunal delivery,
sharpshooters step 387
half an hour after midnight, or 30 minutes from start
of day
1:00 a.m. = 01:00: Retrieve parchment scrolls,
Louvre, Oriental Antiquities, what's left of it
one hour from start of day
6:30 a.m. = 06:30: Check on prisoner, Champs-Élysées,
terrace above the door
6 hours and 30 minutes from start of day:
12:30 p.m. = 12:30: Statements from Duty Guards
regarding Prisoner's Health: Place du Tertre
12 hours and 30 minutes from start of day
4:30 p.m. = 16:30: Prepare Execution Chamber, Hall of
Mirrors, Château de Versailles
16 hours and 30 minutes from start of day
8:15 p.m. = 20:15: Transport Prisoner, second shift:
Sorbonne, École Normale Superieure
20 hours and 15 minutes from start of day
11:59 p.m. = 23:59: Report to Tribunal upon
completion: satellite transmission: S.B. Castle
23 hours and 59 minutes from start of day

12 a.m. = 24:00: Accept Report from Cleanup Crew:
Bastille Métro, Line 5 Platform, direction Bobigny-
Pablo. No sign of the prisoner. All alerts forbidden.
24 hours since start of day, so the end of the day.

*Handwritten notes, reconstructed months later, after—*

# THE DEATH OF BARTHOLOMEW, UNCONFIRMED

Outside the walls of the city, boys sang,
*In this harvest we have yet to reap, turn,*
*turn, your golden key, Bramah, descend,*
*swallow the fires that ravage our lands.*

When he heard these words, Bartholomew fell,
his knees skinned on the ancient stone pavement.
With one hand close to his heart, he said,
*Run, run, find Bramah, bring her to us.*
These were the last words of Bartholomew.

♛

Outside, ghost settlers, remnants of the Resistance,
      a handful of scattered Seed Savers
sang this dirge:
     *Everything is pain, how frail our bodies*
     *bone to liquid, membrane dividers, gone*
     *translucent, bruised, blood, pooling underneath*
     *brown skin yellowed, pulled over lungs reaching*
     *breath by breath laboured, still loving the light.*

The Guard nodded and said, *It were his heart.*

No one believed him for a minute.
Saved by the Save On Children, hands full,
we fled bombardment, camped in the deli.
Pocket knives, cast-off hammers, pried tinned goods,
grocery store produce, Ambrosia apples,
shipped in before supply chains cut, goods lost.
Taught by our parents never to throw seeds.
All roads leading in the end to this place.

The place where we last said goodbye, our gaze
fixed not on the open gate, past the path,
our hands not touching iron or copper
keys left on a parapet of granite,
ice sheets crystallized, sparkling in the sun.
We carried him to the Hidden Valley.

### As Found by the Resistance, Months Later

In the hours before dawn, they render me to a transport plane. They laugh
and say we're going to eat a fine meal in a good restaurant. They speak to
me in a mix of French, Arabic, Mandarin and English. Deserter Guards
who've switched sides many a time. Consortium to Sherronda then back
again to Consortium. I am paying this scribe to write these notes. The
restaurant turns out to be a detention centre. Cries and whispers. If only
I might find again somewhere, somehow, an android to tap out a text. No
way to reach outside. Some kind of cursed, broken-down portal place in
the year 2030. Wait, there's a sound! A key turning in the lock. Who will
be left to know, to tell this story?

♛

*Postscript by Bartholomew,*
*reluctant leader, once scholar,*
*as found, after his trial,*
*from his Before-Time Notes*

Sherronda said to me once, about means
      justifying ends. She was that hard.

*Fragments found inscribed on a scrap of parchment, blowing in the wind:*

——who wrote while awaiting execution.
——to a Catholic church in the Old City.
     ——execution style, one shot, face down first.

♛

# DEFEAT OF THE SWORDS AT THE HANDS
## OF THE MAGNOLIA BRIGADE

A short film by R & G Enterprises
Commissioned by: Consortium at Sherronda's suggestion

Our breast pockets stitched with the name Defarge
White cloths wrapped round our foreheads, voices hoarse
*Sherronda, Captain, Our Captain*
Marching, we laughed at their labels for us:
> *Ici, sans-culottes. Mais oui!*
> *Urban and militant, si!*
Centres crisscrossed we inhabited margins.
To the rostrum to speak, then out to the streets!
Insta anonymous, user tags staged.
> *Ici, sans-culottes. Mais oui!*
> *Urban and militant, si!*
Action, camera, lights. Our knives and our guns.
Reports and memoirs, newspaper accounts.
Our scissors and our knitting needles, hacked.
> *Ici, sans-culottes. Mais oui!*
> *Urban and militant, si!*
Microchips implanted to know our thoughts.
We pledged to Sherronda, we'd cut them out
by any means necessary, shorn skulls
ready to storm barricades, ready to die.
> *Sherronda, Captain, Our Captain*
Our intensity a furious cauldron.
Who could resist us?
Those high-born women, their lily-white skin.
> *Swords! Where are your songs for the Seasons—now?*
> *Hunger tramples nostalgia, we march on!*

Our hands stronger from years of Patch 'n Mend.
You forgot what it's like, forgot to bend.
Our knees bloodier, your time here will end.

*Rogue posting on an outlier Cy-Board: Raphael's Lament*

[Deleted by Sherronda]

# SHERRONDA BETRAYED BY HER OWN MERCENARIES

*Sherronda's last words before the Battle of the Far Plains:*
[Unverified, disputed and unacknowledged]

### Time Is Like a Bad Game

first you want it to speed up.
Youth's desire: to be allowed
    to do things, like an adult,
        you can't, you won't wait.
Then Time laughs, sets the play for real
    and lets you figure out:
        one bad knee, one hip askew,
he's got you on the Finite Plan.

### Overheard Outside Sherronda's Encampment

Safe inside her draperies, curved waist lost.
Once, Sword Girl, now Consortium Elite,
agreements signed, death notices hidden.

### Sherronda's Magnolia Brigade Marched Ever Westward

*Come along then, Shanti-Ben, born to rule.*
*Your thin bones covered, your hard face, polished.*
*Come along then, Shanti-Ben, we'll follow you forever.*
Their faces impassive, their feet in rags.

## THE ARREST OF SHERRONDA, GI OF THE GREEN ZONE

Tribunal C——That cannot be; plus, your demotion, permanent.

Sherronda——I deny everything and for all time——

Tribunal C——Your date of execution to be determined——

Sherronda——This is true. Also, we'll see——

Tribunal C.——Well. We all have our ways and means.

Sherronda——*Je reviens!* And my sword will be a scourge upon——

        Two Guards, laughing and coughing, struck her down.


As Reported to the Committee of Public Safety
Under Direct Orders of Consortium

Let all records show the soldier Sherronda, removed from high office.
Stripped of all titles, compensation for service declared null and void.

As Recorded in the Accounts of Q1, Tribunal HQ

To be paid out, for services rendered, R & G Enterprises.
No currency available but let the record show a promissory note.

Published in the *Consortium Gazette*

Bots, coders, cash to book, desperate entry
rituals to endlessly refresh a screen
illegal overstayers, visas, done.
Guards of the Fifth Gate recruited in droves.
Bookings disappearing, within seconds.
Refresh, refresh, scan for available.
No time to click through, site watchers declined.
Outside Perimeter's Big E, passwords
duplicated. Wireless signals, jacked.
Big bucks and waitlists, passports and long lines.
Forgers, middle folk, a brisk barter charged.
Tips swapped on illegal, short-term websites.
Self-isolated and alone, no luck.
All sector supply chain breakdowns, bombed trucks.


*Let all evil die and the good endure*

# SODDEN PARCHMENT SCRAPS TRAMPLED UNDERFOOT

*They filled our bee boxes—they slashed our hives—*
*we'll come back—in twenty-five-nine-two-oh*
*—and shake, soils into space, water pressure*
on and tight, tilt and slide, rupture, great waves—
*Come ye in, airborne,* they whispered lips bled,
after, *masks and hoods, masks and hoods.*

And came then to a grove of oak trees, sighing,
*Poisoned water in this well, all are dying.*

We walked the circle without a true wish.
All taken from us, joker to queen, bits
of paper, from the Before-Time, fluttering——

When we looked up, pages as leaves fell down
inscribed in the faintest brown lettering
gathering as fast as we could, crumbling
fragments pieced together in that dark wood.

Honeyed brown S-curves, undulating shape
Sonali the Golden, sly, beauty made
well before her sister, Abigail-ji
lost, hurled down the Portal of Wind and Rain.
Sonali, Sonali, father unknown
when oak turns to russet, you'll find her here
honey-locust green shading to golden.
Sherronda, your mother, she'll outwit men
Sonali, Sonali, father unknown
when oak turns to russet, you'll find her here.

Around us the air vibrated, hissing,
*Sisters not by blood!*

*Buckleberry Ferry, Brandywine Bridge,*
croaked the fortune teller with a sly grin.
*Precession & ecliptic, she'll come back.*

*Take a step back,* said Rajancrantz.
*I'm already there,* said Gabbarbhai.

# THE VANISHING OF RAJANCRANTZ & GABBARBHAI

We knew to play the cards.
We saved lost transcripts, useful in negotiations.
We succeeded in advance recruitment and retention,
     Guards drifting back for higher wages.
Consortium approved. They gave us one tattered cloak.
Stitched inside torn cotton seams this sign:
*RHRF* ♛
and a small packet of non-GMO seeds.

We gave Consortium everything we could.
We gave over Sherronda's command.
We knew to leave no trace save a burial mound.
     Film cannisters.
     One inscription, outer rim.
     *Let all evil die.*

## The Restoration, 2108

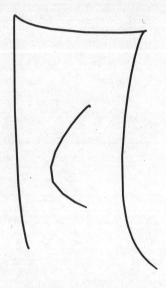

## AS WITNESSED

Exquisite graffiti inscribed on Perimeter walls. Visible only at midnight,
or in the hours before dawn, glimmering red and black.

     Their limited and oh so correct State of Emergency.
     Their virtual virtue,
           eager to acknowledge other peoples' land.
Their wellness
Their electric cars
Their hydroponic
Their solar-wind machines
Their Big E ration cards
Their electronic gadgets
Their sleek computers, always on, no time stamps
Their wireless networks, unlimited
Their Executives, brand-name watches, glowed
        blue-black, their worth and value, overpriced.
Good family men, they provided the best
        resort holidays and platinum finds.
Pandemics and wildfires neutralized.
Wealth, its own antidote to rapid change.

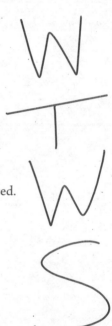

Outside Perimeter, we hunted shade
lined up for water, wireless access.
Transit riders we rode into their Luxe:
        stood dutifully, serving at dinner.
Our tattered Guild-Making skills, half-forgotten
crafted to capture the Moon, her sly smile
mistress mocking our attempts at return
stowaways aboard Private Transport Planes
we hid from chain-ganged *Free-Ds*, their slogans
stitched inside old cotton T-shirts.

*Freedom*: they'd harangue anyone nearby.
Consortium kept us all prisoners in fear.
*Chaos is Bad for Business*, they all said.
We stole glances at the Free-Ds, bereft
their fuel cans removed by Consortium.
Grandmother's warnings rattled in our brains:
*Beware the Free-Ds, destitute, desperate.*
Alas, all of us trapped together now—

## THE GOOD LIFE .2

Prized private, the last preserved stands of oak
thousands of leaves to be painted, falling——
Smooth white faces in our electric cars
free trade zones, robust. Container shipping
redesigned, carbon emissions reduced.
Brisk business for tax credits and Bitcoins.
Wind and solar private stocks, earnings high.
Inside Perimeter, big box normal.
Tribunal letters releasing captives.
Consortium stockholders' approval gained.
welcomed by a phalanx of Fifth Gate Guards.
*Survival of the richest, look away,*
street sweepers sang in the morning, rueful.
Relief when all the lights got turned back on.
By then we didn't care about two tier.
No shivering on damp ground, no wood to chop!
　　just
gig economies and the Bitcoin blues.
Everyone free to create their own memes.
Our children made do as best they could, schools
ramshackle, textbooks scarce, the lights stayed on.
Field trips to inside Centre C's mansions
holidays, tutors, toys, cakes, clothes, haircuts.
Indentured for years, we said, *Worth the cost.*
Prisoners held without charge, rendered, hidden.
Detention Centre, Cold Rooms re-enhanced.
Taller walls and increased surveillance cameras.
Legal permanent residents exiled.
Outside, street children, roaming with their brooms:
　　　　*Freedom fighter, terrorist*
　　　　*who's right, wrong*
　　　　*we just want to eat*
　　　　*been so long*

Remnants, underground resistance
Garry oaks, we heard of gatherings
island groves, camas lilies at the root.
Dollars strengthened as oil prices rose,
*Nobody saying carbon dioxide!*
Containers, truckers, groceries, short supplies.
Still, we didn't dare complain all things being
    equal. *No going back*, we said, and turned——
dialling down the sun, welcoming the night.
   *International stars*
   *performing at the highest level*
   *fulfilling their brightest dreams*
Loud speakers, central square, Big E cut off
plaza drones shepherding crowds to gather
physical attendance mandatory
spheres of influence, podium scaffolds
everyone stood, listening to the same thing.
Someone, somewhere, heard the fortune teller
*Buckleberry Ferry, Brandywine Bridge,*
raucous voice and an unforgiving grin.
New Consortium edicts: No Repairs.
Clicking and liking, delivery lines
robust, on demand, guaranteed sales.
Clicking and liking, and liking online
global and networked, all back on again.
Maybe some of us sighed in our hearts when
we saw the old bike and typewriter shops.
Patch 'n Mend Brigades fled to the far hills.
Someone, somewhere: a New Executive.

*About the New Consortium Executive*
*———Notes Left Behind by T-LOHK, the Itinerant Scribe*

Tenure secure, he fancied himself an anarchist.
Abhorring waste, he reissued bans on plastic bags.
Ration cards a plenty in his pocket, he preached green.
Pleased and grateful, he circulated widely
determined to remain unvaccinated.
*Cookies and bacon, filched for his children.*
This song overheard outside his mansion.

Up on the hill, that old abandoned well.
No one left to make a wish, no one to tell
    heard only by strangers
    women on the run
    unable to confirm or to deny
    words heard drifting on the edge of a breeze:

*Fear Worry Dread*
    *Carbon filchers spilling*
*Fear Worry Dread*
    *Drought-Famine, Fire-Flood*
*Soon We'll All Be Dead.*

# ONCE WERE CALLED CONQUEROR

October as then was called, dividing
the living from the dead, more diaphanous.
Raphael wrote, crossed out, the word ~~father~~.
Each night he'd stand by the Good-Bye river.
Dimensions thinner, the portal still able to send
and release, chestnut trees and oak, outspreading.
*Winter, spring, summer fall,* the boys sang slow
no longer understanding what the words meant.
*Somewhere we knew mountains and the sea, waiting
we'll come back, we'll come back
in 25,920—in 25,920.*

*It had to be done,* Raphael would say.
*But at what cost?* cried the voices, banished.
Wasteland inhabitants, prophets of his doom.
Looking back on concrete, he regretted
laughter, heart too full of remembrance
he fled, longing forever the hidden oaks
pushed to the outskirts of Perimeter,
where he waited, not a sign or word from Bramah.

*And I know why,* he'd repeat to himself.

No one to believe what he'd become. Informer for Consortium.

The wind sighed with Raphael,

*Once we were together, once we broke bread*

*banished now, the Seasons, calling all the dead.*

## RAPHAEL DETAINED BY CONSORTIUM

So much long-discarded gossip
*This is what happens when you sell your soul.*
So much hearsay
    seared into my heart
    memories, her flashing eyes!

These document keepers, unreliable
their laughter at night in the compound

after prisoners interrogated
inside, the Collect.

Outside, the chanting
*J'accuse! J'accuse!*

Strength to jest
before blows

I've never left this compound.
I read the dust here as library
    where once I lived in concrete quarries.
In a far, forgotten corner of my prison cell
    an old oak box
        side handles carved.
I've heard Guards gossip, what the Tinker said
    him on contract to mend and to barter.
*That box, been there forever, maybe once, even, unlocked.*
*No one but Bramah with a key to turn—*

When the Guards marched Raphael to Detention Centre C,
    Beggars shouted, *blicket auf!* But no one did.

# RAPHAEL RESCUED FROM DETENTION CENTRE C

*As found later, prison cell empty, walls stencilled in red and black:*


Wood Stone        Metal Bone

Amber Cloth       Feathers Furs

Iron Salt         Soapstone Tin

> *Meet me in the middle then*
> *sad-eyed, dusty and——*

Secret prisoner, driven to the forest
midnight, a cover, dawn's breaking, assigned
black soil hurled into large pits, avoided
blindfolds untied, Bramah's hands, unshackling—
code breaker of Consortium ciphers
traced palimpsest edges, fragments, margins
almost unseen, nearly forgotten, yet
she figured out the how-tos, studied maps
wiped from the face of the earth, erasure
unseen save for those who knew how to look
messages delivered, bark furrowed days.
Raphael and a small girl—Sonali,
saved.
Raphael looked down at Sherronda's girl.
Daughter by another man, yet still his.
Her large brown eyes looked up; parched mouth open
silent and not cowering, she waited.

# SURVEILLANCE FOOTAGE FOUND BY CONSORTIUM

Portals wide open, Seasons disarrayed
Battleground pitched mid-afternoon, wind, rain

Raphael grasped his daughters' hands, eyes closed
Not the praying kind he fervently prayed

Abigail-ji, youngest, screaming, *Father!*
Her sleek black head, her tremulous eyes

small brown hands wrenched, cyclone savage furies
screeching their demands, atonement for loss——

of a thousand species, of herbs and grasses
of temperate days, long, leisurely summers

Sonali the Golden adopted girl
Raphael meant to hang on but could not——

Spinning away ever faster, hurled fast
*V*-shaped time disrupter, nothing to last

She told us to remember everything
She warned us that each event might shift, change
She told us we'd nod our heads, then forget

Packet to packet, chestnut tree crevice
Raphael and his daughters: names, etched, saved
whispered, word of mouth, tree finds, wrapped rags
steps forward into the future, rubbed held
Faint echoes ringing, Beggars and Swords sang:

Right as rain, good as new
Jumped the Fence, you should too—

Jumped the Fence, you should too—
        Hey, now Bramah, come along

            The one you search for
He'll not wait long

        You'll find him in Consortium Concrete
                sad-eyed, loquacious,
        dusty and strong!

# CONSORTIUM'S RESTORATION SONG

*Nothing rugged or torn, nothing patched brown*
*Everything light, smooth, shiny, strong and new*

Document Retrieval:
Six Months into Their Restoration

Force-fed fury, the winds of November
elongated months as if forever
Dark mornings slits of light, evening to night
Troubadours banned from singing of the sun
Lost Big E ration cards, hot market trade
food prices, oil and gas, water lines cut
threshold winters, before the big one struck
Consortium intent on New Normal
Reserve army of labour, global hires
eBay to Bitcoin, the latest Androids
Perimeter executives clicking
late night expensive goods forward travel
private space flights booked, while we stood waiting——

Farmers in the fields, GMO crops, yield.
Everyone wanting things to stay the same.

As Recorded by Consortium, Outside Perimeter

Flayed alive by existence, we walked on
frayed nerve endings exposed to the north wind
memories cutting crosswise, we hauled water—
mornings, the Well gave what she could stagnant.
If by fog or mist, faint, we might hear, what?
No, we couldn't reckon with imaginings.
We learned to re-boil, beat copper, two tins
cold drove us to efficiency, two sticks
rubbed as taught, wisps of smoke, the first signs, watched.
Words arrived, packet to packet, tree-placed
crevices, where fingers grasped, stained parchment scraps.
Hands stiff and trembling, we traced words, symbols
         —the fire and the rose—

*Whimsical*, most of us said, turning heads
eyes downcast, jaws set, still we waited——
No one brave enough to say her name loud.
Nonchalance a ruse for what sang inside.

Bramah! Come to us with your lock and key

♕ ♕ ♕

*The Tale of the Disappeared Beggar Boy and His Sequoia Seeds*

The seeds, if held, warmed, then crushed with a smooth basalt stone at the night of the first moon. The wish, if sincere, of transference: if you were feeling really sad about some really terrible thing. The rubbing, and the stone, the chanting and the words, joy-bringers, the worse your predicament, the better you'd feel, the more the magic would take hold. No words necessary. How could there be with a boy who never spoke. His vibrations pure, simple, telegraphing the location of Raphael, grown to rue his love, sure to swim in an ocean of regret. Abigail's son, mind! From that whirlwind of time, the dust of Consortium Concrete, a light powder when Bramah whisked him up and away. And not him alone! For his heart took pity on the girl left behind, Sonali, motherless. What price did Bramah ask? *Let all evil die and the good endure.*

But chance and fate intervened. Raphael saved and the Beggar Boy, prisoner of the Eternal Game where play he must, forever to save us from rising seas and eternal scorching winds, all green gone, all soil blown away. There he sits, in the Court of Al-Rashid, chess pieces moved, one century at a time.

*Consortium posted notices*
*as circulated by the Magnolia Brigades*
*        now hired, contracted by the hour*
*to scour every nook and cranny outside Perimeter*

Limited Access Only
Authorized Maps Must Be Used.
Access to Oak Trees, Restricted.
Shiva Calendars Banned.
No Portal Hopping Permitted.

*Hidden Valley,* a phrase rarely spoken.

TALES OF THE SEASONS, BANNED

*Bramah told us—*

    Memorize each taproot
        . your feet and your hands to find what words won't——
    spruce, chestnut, two cherry trees and six oaks
        a plane tree and a beech—

*Bramah taught us—*

    how to stay safe, hidden because unseen,
        bus riders, silent our shopping bags full
    how we'd sit in the dawn's early light
        them cleaning trains, shiny electric, copper
        handled to chrome surfaces, smooth gliders.

*Bramah, we sighed—*

    they keep us in reserve, to care for, to clean
        their children fed, ours, to fend as best we can

    only ever be—although sometimes we dream—
    Perimeter rebuilt with gates and locks, opening—

*How much time left?*
We asked the wave-crested sea.
We taught our own to sing:

this present, that is our future
*We'll come back—in twenty-five-nine-two-oh*
*We'll come back—in twenty-five-nine-two-oh*

# *Bramah at the Portal of the Lost Seasons*

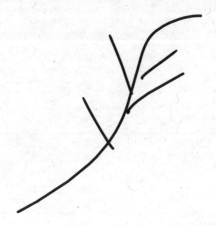

ESCAPE TO THE HIDDEN VALLEY

Before-Time trucks, cars rushing down Boundary
used to be Price Park, Before-Time playground
eastside, used to be the Battle of Kingsway
all the children long gone, their parents, too
in the Wet and the Dry, only the oaks
and them too, gnarled, diseased, still with a tap
and a watch, and a step, portals remaining lost, forgotten
          but not quite——

Crown of blanched leaf stems, old roots, the air warm
lone chickadee, calling *fee-bee*, two notes
suspended. Fragrance, a hawthorn message
undeliverable. Time, a lost sender.

Remnants of the Resistance, carried seeds.
Bark furrows, lichen-laced, Sakura loss.
Encoded in ridges, scant leaves fell
centuries-old machine guns, still reliable.
All-walkers, we pressed wet felt on our feet.
Found blowing in the wind, from a notebook
          by the Itinerant Scribe T-LOHK
last seen waiting for Bramah at the Portal of the Lost Seasons
          before his heart exploded, Bartholomew the Good
          bright bird's morning song, six-petalled lotus
          timbre, texture, his voice from the Before
          passages through, memory a springtime bell
                    echoing; time's golden thread, knotted, pulled—
          doors locked, unlocked, gates swinging toward
          back-stopped to memory, a hinge
          tended or forgotten, numbers stone carved
          cut lines, grooves, chiselled surfaces brushed fine
          arrow quivering, black earth, furrowed ground.

Almost to miss the Portal Opening, Wet
Dry, the need to stay still, also to move
mushrooms clinging to trunks, cedar, chestnut
oak leaves withering, falling, who would know
to knock, fingers a-holding bark, feet sunk
moss cups, acorns, our gaze sweeping upwards.
*Draco in three thousand,* we swore stars sang
Before-Time sirens, wailing into dusk
threshold discovery, *Vega in twelve.*
This present, that is our future
and we went forward, saying, *We'll come back*——
*in twenty-five-nine-two-oh,* and then Bramah——
one last look, she stood, Portal Threshold, raised
embedded in, surrounded by, birdsong.

# BRAMAH'S QUEST CONTINUED

>>>>>>
♛ ♛ ♛


Heard in villages, towns and the Great Cities of Transaction
      heard far and wide, on trains, under bridges
           transport riders, chain-ganged, they'd sing of the day
*Overhand, cross, underhand, push, pull——pull*
*only Bramah's hands deft enough to turn*
*left, half-circle, click, then turn right, open—*
*Bramah knew not to disturb the gods' play*
*boules, checkers, shuffleboard, long games of chess*
*laughter made their malice-moves, thunder, clicks!*
*Turn left, half-circle click; then, right, open—*
Gold lock, bronze key, twigs snapped under her feet.
Moonlight caught Orion's Belt sparkling, south.
Guild Hall workers on strike, a thousand days.
Seamstresses marching across factory floors.
Somewhere a lone dog barks, rooftop peddler
lanky with a side smile, and a nod, plays
melodies from Before-Times, distant years
accumulating back and forth, clouds drift.
Midnight's Threshold: she knows to pause and wait;
treasure trove, sealed vaults, strands of DNA.
Antarctica expedition, lost archives
temple cloths from Ahmedabad, Baghdad
gates open, courtyards stained with blood, washed clean.
Her Pippin file, delicate, painted green.

### Said Bramah as She Worked

Carriers who brought me to this planet.
Others might sigh and say: *Mother, father.*
Legacy in the faintest letterings—
although I found within a new motto:
*Let all evil die and the good endure*
Behind the words, galaxies of nuance
gestures and palimpsest, not set aside.
Tools in hand, I turn a lock. I hear—
*Fare Forward, Voyagers!* Hope against the odds,
stacked troubles, no one for, still; to go on——
birth and death eliding those Four Seasons
mother, father gone—once rose, once fire
and still to go on, making my own time.
My key and my lock, gold, silver and bronze.
Finger to thumb, straight edge rasp, stroked thin, rubbed
liftoff in seconds, she knew to slow Time:
hands, pocket bound, to pull out a chalice
miniature instruments, a magic oak box
methodical, slow, minute and precise
each turn, then click, and turn again, open:
six supernaturals, Bramah knew to call
signs and symbols; fire, earth and water
in the next dimensions, oak box to locks,
the Golden Cloth of Samarkand,
  *My quest continues,* she sang to herself,
    *to find the truth about my origins.*

♛ ♛ ♛

>>>>>>

ANONYMOUS POSTS, CY-BOARD #10

## Bramah's Treatise on the Humans

Where language began, contiguous edge,
they sensed side-by-side, dissonant power.
To take and then to take again, without
replenishment; to overfish, fallow
fields not left to rest, to modify seeds.
Dissonant power, speaker after speaker
asserting rights, their demands without care.
Arguments marshalled, settlers' advantage
always to spot the main chance, get, get, spend.
Quick to stake a position, insistent
explanations, rationale, systems, maps.
Everything made sense, hardened into grids.
Dollar signs added to excellent trades.

\*

## Bramah Teaches Us the Resistance

We, silent, made things, heads bent, hands at work.
We watched to see how the land was taken
We remained composed, the clay and the wheel.
We spoke prophecy with unease growing.
Birds piped the dawn—sun no longer benign
Story keeping its secrets tucked away
Treasure trove discovered, all the untold
Bramah stood and stared out the vast unlocked
        Fragments from the past, leather-bound notebooks.
    When we bent our heads to hear, she said,
        *Find a vista from which to see the world*
                *waiting——*

347

# *At the Gate of the Fisherman's Knot*

# BETWEEN TIME'S DIMENSIONS

*and step——*

No one left to recall the Four Aunties.
Not one brick uncracked at the Wishing Well

came the times and they were bad, Dry to Wet
obsessed with higher ground and no regrets

starved for shade, when drought struck, roaring flames licked
parched soil blown thin, cascading mud and slick.

Faster the cycle of Dry to Wet
unpredictable veering forward and back.

No chance to plan, only react, desires
simple: what once was four by four and twelve.

We closed our eyes, we called for Bramah's key
our feet dragged thresholds, one last look, and then

gold and green and in-between and never
who will believe us, chained to forever——

# GHOST HOLOGRAM

>>>>>>

### *Once Were Called Raphael the Conqueror*

We found him in Consortium Concrete
sad-eyed, loquacious, dusty and strong-armed.

He worked the night shift and those Sword Girls teased,
*Hey Rafe, keep talking you'll never beat us,*

bed to lips, your warm stories, our cold hands
anyways, your mouth always moving, strange

orange flickers in rusted cans, your tales—
*Hey Rafe, sharpen your point, jab us again,*

laughing and lethal, they danced as he spoke.
Let it be said that he never won once.

Many a girl who tried to teach him joust.
Many an old woman who loved his words.

Wolves howled on the battlefield when he fell.
See him here before you, his songs to tell.

## THE GREAT SHIP FORWARD

There's a ship they call *The Great Year Forward*.
She's waiting on the tarmac, but not for long!
   Old 747, galley-birthed
she'll take us there, she'll bring us back, circling
the sun, the moon, the stars, Vega, Draco
our oars, jet engines, the last of the fuel.

There's a ship and she's all our own, waiting
Draco in three thousand, Vega in twelve
     in twenty-five-nine-two-oh
she'll take us there, she'll bring us back, circling.
Come, Bramah find your past, oak and cedar
they won't last, oh the sun, the moon, the stars
this old plane she's heading out, find us, fast——

Bramah, you'll have till the year's midnight hour
     O Precession and Ecliptic, away
       toward, the great year and the great circle.
     Equinox, Solstice, together, apart——
Away, toward, Beggars and Swords lament
branded and bartered, their shoulder tattoo
     red inked to fade, daytime to shade, hurry
Bramah, look for the signs and turn your key
     O Precession and Ecliptic, away
       toward, this ship ever ready but not for long.
This planet tilting, the great shift coming—

she'll take us there, she'll bring us back, circling
when we come back sure as this world spins fast.
*Vega to Draco, in twenty-five-nine-two-oh*
*When we'll come back, in twenty-five-nine-two-oh*

## TRANSPONDER 25,920: SONGS OF THE VOYAGE

As handed down, migrant to Seed Saver
bits and pieces as memory served:

divining wheel, a thousand threads entwined.
     Before, every door, every key thrown, every gate locked

forward, backward, a thousand needles cleaned.
Our hands in the Before-Time, thread to loom
· our eyes sparkled, names embossed, cut, held.
*Distance and a centre, homecoming bound*
Oak leaf in first bud, honey locust, too.
Unfurled lime green, we'd come to rue the day
     portal fences, we'd jump by chance or fate
     hologram disks snatched, or bits of parchment.

*as inscribed by T-LOHK,*
*partial transmission, of an un/known survivor*
>>>>>>

Kingsway and Melbourne, November 26, 2021
Pandemic Year 1.11, in between three atmospheric rivers
walking up Melbourne, I saw the BBQ House, used to be
the Samosa Gardens. Used to be years and a day
in the year of the reign, hologram and counting
     2001 >>>>>> ·
     last minute invites to my fortieth birthday party,
my own mum and dad, the years between us
    I wasn't sure I even wanted—hard to think
       hard to accept: it were one of the last times
    I saw them together, three months later
       dad would be dead, it were that April
       the worst portal taking ever—I walk up the hill

steep step to breath, counting the years and a day,
one scratch on this disk
memories returning mobile
could this walking bring spirits back to this hill
would I have thought then, at forty
that I would be walking up these hills
this valley, this other side—the last
known portal.

Consortium hire, I've only words
handed-down songs and found parchment letters
the last of the elderly from the Before
wheelchair-bound, their hands trembled, feet swollen
abandoned, nearly forgotten care homes
they made me recite; they made me write down:

## Of Weather

*Atmospheric* we were taught to say, drenched
dreams of grey skies supplanting piercing blue.
Hearts broken, parched land, we waited for rain.
Heavy constant straight downpours, sheets buckets
blankets bubbling sluiced rivulets to streams.
Only then we learned the Bridgehead extreme.
Our earth's internal mechanism, jammed
stuck on hazardous, no more temperate.
Farewell to predictable and moderate.
Buffeted Dry to Wet, no in-between.
Mornings we'd lie under leaking rooftops
counting past portals where Seasons behaved.
Not about our desires, we learned late.
Lost threshold children, standing at the gate.

♛

## Of the Journey & the Quest

Sailmaking, dyes and twisting lengths of rope:
in the end, memory found the simplest one
overhand, cross, underhand, push, pull——pull
*Turn left, half-circle click; then, right, open—*

Bramah found her people, Grandmother's threads
    of Bartholomew the Good, heartache, unending
    of Raphael, sad-eyed, doomed, still rescued
    of his daughters, one lost, one saved, Sonali
        echoing the mockery of her flawed mother
            Sherronda, saviour and destroyer
            her flashing eyes! her snake-coiled hair!
    of the Beggar Boy, destined now to play
        the forever game, piece by piece, saved queen
            king eternally moved in the Court of Al-Rashid
            Lost Portal of the Four Seasons
*Let checkmate never be heard,* called Bramah
        to banish ground ozone, to stave off extinction
        to ice eternal on the East Antarctic Shelf——
Time's span, a fortnight, none left to play games
chance, fate, a roll of dice, crowds turned to mobs
Big E monitors when available
lower case and anonymous postings
demanded more or negotiated less, rules
supply-side contracts, bonus arrangements.
Impossible to keep up with demand.

A plane tree and a beech—six oaks and two cherry trees
fragments of an old box, frayed rope undone
*Once was a house much loved, them hard times,*
        warriors to sing, to find the stars at night
        compass, caravel and astrolabe prized

of the seeker, Bramah, what of her own origins?
That old oak box! That disappearing document!
Still searching, still to come——

♛

### Of the Seed Savers

Gather in the clearing, rain or sunshine
bare feet on the roots of the Mother Tree
who will count Seasons, o'er this earth of mine.

Gather in the clearing, sunshine or rain
hacked if by hand saw, then save seeds for our pain.
Remember the rhythm of our thresholds.

Hands to the winds, eyes to the stars, look up!
Winter, spring, summer or fall, gather seeds.
Troubadours from every epoch knew us.

Gather in the clearing, rain or sunshine.
When droplets do not burn when drought is gone.
Last generation to remember us.

Our seeds in glass jars, the Wet or the Dry.
Beans, squash, roses and corn, beggars will cry:

> wishes, wishes
> well over time
> prayers for rain
> planting by sun
> *un coup de dés*
> *jamais, jamais*

Rentalsman in ruins, vagabond children
they run faster than any increment
climate disasters clinging to their heels.

*Jumped the Fence, did you?*
*We did, too.*

Pinched faces, staring eyes, still they stand proud.
*I am here,* Bramah will say. *All will be well.*
We will bend our heads low; we dare not tell——

**Transmission Intermittent: >>>>>>**

Some said, *Bramah seen with the Sifting Sisters.*
Some said, *by an old abandoned Wishing Well,*
        *Portal of the Lost*

**Dear Future Survivors, These Last Images**

Rentalsman Unit, bombed-out roof
patched over with tarp, wind-snapped gap, where hands sift for eternity
clearing papers, touching old family photographs
Polaroid snapshots fingered
black and white paper, scalloped edges in white
vinyl-covered albums, stacked vertical in a faux-wood shelf
water-stained and mouldy, sticky, pulled apart
placed with care in paper bags—in the distance between
faint echoes heard, Beggars and Swords
        *Un coup de dés, jamais jamais*
reserve armies of labour chained and marching
        for the next transport plane, the next cycle—

♛ ♛ ♛

two rats skittered across white withered grass
city plane trees dropped their leaves, once deep green.

♛ ♛ ♛

## MEANWHILE ON PLANET EARTH

Cleanup crew left behind, the darkest hue
       shipped in or on transport planes, migrants too
hired on contract by Consortium
       air quality monitors non-functional.

### *We Sing Bramah's Questing Song*

Jump the fence, roll the dice, find the oak trees
Hidden Valley shimmering between worlds
banyan to maple, cotton to silk, luck!
Golden key in Bramah's hands unlocking
*tales within tales, chalice,* the old well sighed.
How the bees hummed with Bramah's fingers, quick,
turning to click, then run, to find again—
*I'll find them again; I'll tell them to run.*
*Overhand, cross, underhand, push, pull——pull*
We'll wait as we wander, we'll save all seeds.
*Come Bramah, in the street that time forgot*
trees without leaves, intimation of green
wind lifting, water's edge, brown river god,
*Shanti-Ben vanquished, Bramah,* sight unseen.

*Un coup de dés, jamais jamais,*
*of Precession and Ecliptic, Jump the Fence*
*point of no return,* we sang soft and slow.
Come now, you Aunties, come now to find
sharpen our swords, sweep up our sticks.

*No going back to Before, fare forward.*
Come now you Aunties come all ye down
wish us at the Well, see us to the gate.

*Avalanches, floods, raindrops that will burn.*
Come now Bramah, bring us your lock and key.
Golden the broom, ever green your mystery.

*Fare Forward, Voyagers!*
Faint echoes encircling, Vega's light;
there's a ship and she's all our own, waiting
*Draco in three thousand, Vega in twelve*
*in twenty-five-nine-two-oh (25,920)* ——

### We Find an Old Oak Box, Scarred Lid Inscribed

All things must fade, pass away and return
      green shoots, old wood, acacia, laurel
winter-flowering jasmine, glossy leaves
   luck-bearer if we but pay attention
how to recede from the centre with grace
     who will be left to listen to earth-words
sent in every windstorm, quake, fire, flood
     all things must fade then pass away, return
bring sweet flowering jasmine for good luck
     chance and fate will meet us at this last gate.
Unimaginable distances the past.
Light years forward, then homecoming to earth.

♛

Up by the Wishing Well, blasted and dry
    on the precipice of the unknown
one Pippin file, a broken shoelace, tied
     stencilled, faded, brick worn smooth
        fortune teller with her own palm held open

no one to trace slate to stone, carved letters
  *spruce, chestnut, two cherry trees and six oaks*
  *a plane tree and a beech—arcadia—*


>>>>>>
♕ ♕ ♕

As we walked away, we said:
*After, there's another story we'll tell——*

# A Note to the Reader

Thank you for entering the world of THOT J BAP. I thought you might like to know a little bit more about this world and the goings on inside of it. If you've read Book One of this epic series, you'll know that New Year's Eve holds a special place in my creative practice. It's the ultimate Portal Threshold! Scenes and poetry seem to spill forth, and so it was New Year's Eve, 2021, leading into 2022, at the start of the Omicron explosion. The work continued through all the dire happenings of war, invasion, protests, drought, floods and now, in September, a personal catastrophe for my own family. Through it all, I've been here working on this book. I hope you'll think of THOT J BAP and its characters as I do, true friends to whom you can return. May we all know better, brighter times; may books and story endure. XRSS. Labour Day Monday, 2022.

# LIVES LIVED IN THOT J BAP: BOOK TWO

| Name | Birth | Death | Age at Death |
|------|-------|-------|--------------|
| Bartholomew | 2050 | 2107 | 57[*] (disputed) |
| Sherronda | 2083 | 2108 | 25[**] |
| | | | (also disputed) |
| | | | |
| Raphael | 2084 | | |
| Sonali | 2103 | | |
| Aunty Tabitha | 1995 | unknown | |
| Grandmother | un/known | still alive | |
| Aunty Magda | un/known | still alive | |
| Bramah | un/known | a demigoddess/ locksmith, just beginning to understand her origins. | |

| | |
|---|---|
| Guards of the Fifth Gate | unavailable |
| Beggars | undocumented |
| Swords | sworn to secrecy |
| Magnolia Brigade | decimated in battle; a few survivors form the Cult of Sherronda |
| T-LOHK the Scribe | redacted |

[*] Followers of Bartholomew insist he is still alive, just disappeared.
[**] Cult of Sherronda maintains she is still alive.

# EVENT SUMMARY OF THOT J BAP: BOOK TWO

### Part One: 2087–2105 ~ Bramah's Quest to Find Her People

Bramah's Quest is to find the truth of about her origins and to find her people, last seen at the end of Book One in the year 2087. At that time, Grandmother, the Beggar Boy and Raphael escape the clutches of the evil Consortium with the aid of Bramah who finds them refuge in the Hidden Valley. Bramah then sets out to discover more about her past but is called by Grandmother back to the Hidden Valley. With the help of ghost settlers and Ciswen the Blacksmith of the Winter Portal, Bramah finds Grandmother who shares information that leads Bramah to Raphael. He was born at the very end of Book One, in the year 2087, brought up with Bramah's Grandmother and the Aunties of the Wishing Well, under the illusion that he is an orphan. Raphael is the son of the late Abigail, adopted daughter of the late Dr. A.E. Anderson. Raphael's father is Bartholomew, who escaped Migrant Camp #3.

Part One shows us their world, where accelerated climate change reduces four seasons to three: a brutal and unforgiving Winter, the Wet and the Dry. The effects of this change are made worse by the socio-economic imperatives of the Consortium, whose hold on earth's resources begins to erode. Bramah continues her search for the old oak box, last seen in the "wrong hands" of Consortium. Bramah wants to find the oak box because it has the mysteriously disappearing document that reveals clues to her own origin. Raphael shares stories of his growing years, including the tale of how he once met the Beggar Boy. Alas, the boys fall prey to a rogue portal and the Beggar Boy finds himself caught in an eternal game of chess ordained by the gods to help stave off more climate catastrophes. When Bramah reconnects with Raphael, they set out to find Bartholomew and Raphael accepts that Bartholomew is his father.

*Part Two: 2105–2108 ~ The Rise, Rule and Fall of Bartholomew the Good*

Raphael is eighteen years old in 2105. He and Bartholomew meet Bartholomew's warrior general, the enigmatic Sherronda. They join the Resistance and stage an uprising against the evil Consortium. Raphael falls in love with Sherronda, much to Bartholomew's displeasure and Bramah's unease. Sherronda, brilliant strategist, helps Bartholomew secure victory over Consortium. Bartholomew's rule is established but alas, not for long. Sherronda, impatient for radical change and ambitious, betrays Bartholomew. Raphael sides with Sherronda, and civil war ensues. Consortium exploits their division, and climate change continues to worsen. Sherronda betrays Raphael, Consortium turns on Sherronda and Raphael is arrested. Raphael helps Sherronda's daughter Sonali escape in a secret portal transfer arranged by Bramah. Although decimated, remnants of the Resistance remain vigilant in the Hidden Valley. Bramah's Quest to help save planet Earth, rescue the Beggar Boy and discover the truth about her origins continues.

## A NOTE ON TIME TRAVEL IN THOT J BAP

In the world of THOT J BAP, all action takes place on planet Earth, albeit simultaneously in different time dimensions. Time travel consists of observation only, like watching a hologram or a movie. Time travel is reserved for Certified Travellers, most of whom are on hire to Consortium, usually hunting down resisters. Bramah is a Certified Traveller and finds ways to subvert the terms of her contract to help others. Sometimes, Travellers will fall down Portals, by accident or due to evil forces. In Book Two, rogue mercenaries, Rajancrantz & Gabbarbhai are also time travellers.

♛

Throughout the world of THOT J BAP, we encounter a set of symbols that allude to the game of chess, to bio-contagion and viruses, to bees and to chemistry. Visit the THOT J BAP website and click on the key, using the code 2020, for more information about this epic.

## ABOUT THE POETRY

*Draco in three thousand, Vega in———12*
*in twenty-five-nine-two-oh———25,920*

In the over ten years of working on this epic, THOT J BAP, I've been influenced by hundreds of texts, including time spent with: T.S. Eliot's *The Four Quartets* and *The Wasteland*; Robin Blaser's collected works, *The Holy Forest*; Rachel Blau DuPlessis' *Drafts*, the poems and plays of Bertolt Brecht, and many editions of the work known as *The Arabian Nights*. In this book, I've immersed myself in the works of Milton, principally *Paradise Lost*, plus new translations of Virgil's *Aeneid* (Shadi Bartsch) and Homer's *Odyssey* (Emily Wilson).

Add to these, Wikipedia forays into Vedic scriptures, family gossip about Hindu gods, as well as rereadings of Christina Rossetti, Octavia Butler, and an old red hymnal. Layered into all of that, readings of scientific reports on climate change and government malfeasance (*CIA Torture Report*), and many more documents, including the history of locksmithing, manuals on craft-making, and old instruction books on inventions and astronomy; not to mention mornings when I listened to the podcast series *The Rest is Politics*. (Alasdair Campbell/Rory Stewart)

To all of this, I've brought my obsession with formal poetry and what I call docu-poetics, the breaking apart of text, to create new forms, often in combination with visuals, such as symbols and signs. In Book One, the verse forms highlighted the sonnet and episodic scenes told through madrigals and ballads as well as spells, codes, riddles. In Book Two, the dominant form is a sequence of blank verse long poems, embedded with nested sets of cantos, crafted into one long book poem divided in two parts. Chants, spells, riddles endure.

Threads of the fantastical take me into new ways of seeing the epic, reclaiming, re-interrogating, fairy tales, myths, legends, culture and the Other. The Before-Time now shifting, faster and faster, into the After. The journey continues. ♛

## ACKNOWLEDGEMENTS

Earlier versions of selected poems can be found in the chapbook *Extractions from THOT J BAP* by Nomados Press (2017), with thanks to Meredith Quartermain. If you have a copy, save it! Nomados closed shop this past year. Gratitude.

Thanks to Nightwood Editions for sharing the vision of innovative poetry and beautifully made books: to Silas White for editing and publishing; and to the Nightwood Team (Emma Skagen and Karine Hack) for copy editing with discernment and with precision. Thanks to the gorgeous artwork of Nadina Tandy; the superb book series design by Top Shelf Creative; and the interior book design by Carleton Wilson and Rafael Chimicatti. In a time of many distractions and "fast food" products, how restorative to work with those who believe in making things to stand the test of time.

Love and gratitude to my husband: he took the time, in a pandemic, to read all of this epic. His unwavering support and enthusiasm helps sustain this journey. Deep thanks to all the readers, micro-publishers, poets and writers, for embracing this work.

Gratitude to the independent publishers and literary journals of Canada for their continued support of long form poetry.

♛ ♛ ♛

## DEDICATION

for my sister, my only sibling,
     for my aunties and my uncles,
          for my mother, fierce warrior,
          made wordless, surviving in this world,
          then taken to the next—
*Fare Forward, Voyagers!*

PHOTO CREDIT: Sandra Vander Schaaf

## ABOUT THE AUTHOR

Renée Sarojini Saklikar is the author of five books, including the award-winning *children of air india* and *Listening to the Bees*. Her poetry, essays and short fiction have appeared in many anthologies and literary magazines, including *Those Who Make Us: Canadian Creature, Myth, and Monster Stories* (Exile Editions, 2016), *Chatelaine*, *The Capilano Review* and *Pulp Literature*. *Bramah's Quest* is the latest volume of her epic fantasy in verse, THOT J BAP, The Heart of This Journey Bears All Patterns. She was poet laureate for the City of Surrey 2015–2018 and volunteers for *Event* magazine, Meet the Presses collective, Surrey International Writers' Conference and Poetry in Canada. Renée Sarojini teaches creative writing and editing at Kwantlen Polytechnic University and hosts Lunch Poems at SFU.